VGM Opportunities Series

OPPORTUNITIES IN
PUBLIC RELATIONS
CAREERS

160201

Morris B. Rotman

Revised by
Luisa Gerasimo

Foreword by
Robert W. Galvin
Chairman, Executive Committee
Motorola Inc.

 **VGM Career Books**

Library of Congress Cataloging-in-Publication Data

Rotman, Morris B.
    Opportunities in public relations careers / Morris B. Rotman. — Rev. ed. / revised
by Luisa Gerasimo.
        p. cm. — (VGM opportunities series)
    Includes bibliographical references.
    ISBN 0-658-01632-6 (hardcover)
    ISBN 0-658-01633-4 (paperback)
        1. Public relations — Vocational guidance.   2. Public relations — Vocational
guidance — United States.   I. Gerasimo, Luisa.   II. Title.   III. Series.

HD59 .R68 2001
659.2'023'73 — dc21

                                                                          2001 17544

Published by VGM Career Books
A division of The McGraw-Hill Companies.
4255 West Touhy Avenue, Lincolnwood (Chicago), Illinois 60712-1975 U.S.A.
Copyright © 2001 by The McGraw-Hill Companies.
Printed in the United States of America
International Standard Book Number: 0-658-01632-6 (hardcover)
                                                  0-658-01633-4 (paperback)

1   2   3   4   5   6   7   8   9   0   LB/LB   0   9   8   7   6   5   4   3   2   1

CONTENTS

Comparison to the field of advertising. The marketing aspect. Reaching a diverse public. Media relations. Development of the public relations industry. The PR person today.

The roots of the profession. Propaganda and public relations. Public relations in the United States. Public opinion in the 1800s and early 1900s. The onset of big business publicity. Expected growth of the field.

Politics. Newspapers. Television. Social activist concerns. Education. Entertainment. Sports. Health care.

Opinion polls. An educated populace. Relating to hostile publics.

ABOUT THE AUTHOR

Morris B. Rotman, APR, is a veteran public relations counselor and former Chicago journalist. He served as consultant to several large corporations and as an adjunct professor of public relations at the College of the Desert in Palm Desert, California.

He built Chicago-based Harshe-Rotman & Druck, Inc., into an international public relations firm with offices in Chicago, New York, Los Angeles, Washington, DC, and London, England. Following a merger in 1982, the firm became Ruder, Finn & Rotman, Inc., with Rotman serving as president and chief operating officer until he retired from the firm and moved his business base to his home in the California desert.

His original firm, Harshe-Rotman & Druck, was retained by many large corporations and was involved in many major public issues of the day, including two presidential campaigns (Nelson Rockefeller and Adlai E. Stevenson). However, Rotman was most widely known for his relationship with the Academy of Motion Picture Arts and Sciences, in

Hollywood, which stages the annual Academy Awards. He worked on it for more than thirty years despite the fact that he was based in Chicago. It was a record for long-term client relationships in public relations circles. He also enjoyed a counseling relationship with Whirlpool, Inc., which covered a span of nearly twenty-five years.

Mr. Rotman was born in Chicago where he attended Tuley High School, Wright Junior College, and Northwestern University. He began his career in journalism before World War II at the Lerner Newspapers on Chicago's northwest side, progressed through the famed City News Bureau of Chicago, joined the *Chicago Sun,* and during World War II served for one year as editor of the Scott Field, Illinois, *Broadcaster.* At the close of the war he entered the public relations field at the Community War Fund and in 1946 became a partner to William Harshe, taking over the firm after Harshe died in 1949. During the next thirty-five years he built and led Harshe-Rotman & Druck, Inc., in its rise to one of the largest and most capable public relations firms in the United States.

Mr. Rotman has counseled nearly every kind of professional, business, and trade organization during his long career and is the author of dozens of articles, speeches, and chapters in books on public relations. Now a member of the Chief Executives Organization, he has been involved with the Public Relations Society of America and was a national director of the Young Presidents Organization, an international organization of company presidents who are under forty-nine years of age. In the Palm Springs desert, he serves as chairman of another group of sixty graduate YPOers called The Desert Rats.

In addition to his business responsibilities, Rotman spent time as a trustee of Chicago's Roosevelt University and is now an emeritus trustee. He is also a Life Director of The Rehabilitation Institute of Chicago after more than twenty-five years of service as a director. He won several awards for his work in creating better understanding and acceptance of the handicapped in everyday life.

Since the inception of the idea by the late actor-director Sam Wanamaker, Rotman served as an American director of the Shakespeare Globe Trust, which built a replica of the original Globe theater on the west bank of the Thames in London, England.

This edition has been revised by Luisa Gerasimo, a freelance writer living in Wisconsin.

FOREWORD

Many people without training in the field consider themselves somewhat expert in public relations and advertising.
When you stop to think about it, that is not totally irratio-
nal—after all, each of us is the public. We are the target of
the effort of those who seek to inform and shape public
opinion. We know what we like and what we don't like. And
we at least indirectly develop standards, expectations, and
opinions as to what might have been done to have caused
our reaction to be different, or what has caused our receptiv-
ity to have been favorable. Yet finding ourselves in this position may be one of the most dangerous of opinions to hold.
For we are at the greatest risk of not knowing what we do
not know.

It has been my privilege to know a few of the leading public relations executives of the country. I consider Morris Rotman a dean among his peers. A quality that each of these
executives holds, and what Morris Rotman possesses in
abundance, is a love of people and an understanding of
them. I presume there are some people successful in the PR

business who do not necessarily have this genuine affection and empathy for people and who succeed at their level as a function of their expertise at the process. But if I were to advise someone entering the public relations field, I would ask them how deep is their interest in people. How able are they to put themselves in the shoes of those whom they wish to influence for good? I have listened to and watched Morris Rotman work his way through a public relations issue and subject with consummate skill at the processes. But the distinguishing characteristic that added to the worth of what he was bringing to the issue was his intimate knowledge of what was on the mind of the public at that time. What could be realistically offered and reasonably accepted? At all times these well-rooted thoughts were matched against a standard of integrity, for he, as well as anyone I know, realizes that the public will accept only the truth.

This book encourages bright people to consider opportunities in public relations. Those with the most genuine interest in the public will serve those opportunities best.

Robert W. Galvin
Chairman, Executive Committee
Motorola Inc.

ACKNOWLEDGMENTS

I give special thanks to Robert W. Galvin, chairman of the executive committee of Motorola, Inc., for his elegant foreword to this book. I recognize the world beats a path to Bob Galvin's door in search of his attention and time. I am fortunate indeed to have had his friendship. Bob is not only one of the world's great industrial leaders but constantly adds to his burden by taking on enormous tasks in the public interest.

Morris B. Rotman

INTRODUCTION

What does it take to be a public relations specialist? Public relations is based in communication, but it can take a wide array of forms including investor relations, public affairs, corporate communication, employee relations, product or marketing publicity, consumer service, or customer relations. Public relations people need a wide variety of skills because they will likely deal with everything from research and evaluation to writing and emergency response.

Because people today move from one job to another many times over the course of a career or careers, it is important to have knowledge of numerous subjects and be able to adapt to a rapidly changing world. It makes sense to be a jack of all trades *and* to have the specific knowledge of the industry for which you work. Applied psychology and intuition help practitioners evaluate what's going on in people's minds; economic and financial savvy brings an understanding of business; knowledge of foreign affairs and foreign languages bridges the gap between cultures; interest in the arts deepens that individual's personality.

Sociology helps the professional to tune into rapidly changing fads and trends. Messages must continuously appeal to the audiences toward which they are directed, and the process for getting that message across changes from month to month, week to week, even day to day. The general public can be fickle, and the public relations person must adapt to these constantly changing moods and preferences.

A public relations specialist performs many invaluable functions for businesses. The effort is based on expertise and draws from many skills. A public relations person must communicate effectively, write well, and be able to present oral material in a straightforward and interesting fashion. Jargon—language that only experts understand—does not convey information clearly.

The public relations specialist must be a consummate journalist, and he or she must be good as are the best reporters and broadcasters. A highly developed news sense, based on a deep understanding of journalism, remains one of the fundamentals of public relations. News sense is the ability to understand why and how stories are covered in print, broadcast, and specialized media, including trade publications. That's why the most successful people in the field still come from journalism's many branches.

Press relations is the heart of the public relations business. In fact, the general public (composed of distinct, separate publics) perceives public relations mostly through the media. Consequently, public relations firms must have the trust of the press in order to make different kinds of best impressions with different publics. To gain that trust, public relations specialists must deliver facts.

To help corporations deal effectively with the press, the public relations person must stay in step with the times. He or she must serve as the person who comprehends the problems that require communications. Public relations people should try to know what major changes will occur well in advance of when they actually occur.

Media sophistication in this technical world is very great. This is especially true in television and Internet news, with its very strict time limits. Station and network directors and producers choose between equally strong stories for their broadcasts. Some materials that could be shown must be left out. Selectivity becomes all-important, and the public relations specialist plays a key role in deciding what appears in news media and what does not. The professional public relations person cannot dictate what is shown on national or local news, but he or she can suggest possible story angles and subjects. What a public relations expert does and how he or she does it often influences how and whether the client's story gets told.

Public relations is an art used in most areas of our lives. Politicians and political parties, entertainers, medical professional organizations, and major sports teams regularly utilize the skills and techniques of public relations specialists to transmit certain messages or images. Each entity wants to convey a favorable image to those segments of society whose support is needed for the organization to reach its goals.

The message must be appealing and forceful, but, above all, it must be accurate. The days of press-agentry, in the sense of "planting" material in the media, are a thing of the past. Today, truth is the watchword of the public relations profession.

The United States Bureau of Labor Statistics reports that more people are entering the public relations field each year. Although there were barely a few thousand people in the field when I began my career, there are now more than 122,000 people working in public relations. About 13,000 of these are self employed. The four largest firms employ thousands of public relations specialists. In addition, thousands of other people are employed full-time by various corporations, government agencies, and associations to represent them in this burgeoning field. Over the years the number of females entering the field has increased dramatically. More than one-half the number of people in PR are women.

Perhaps you, too, can become a public relations person and enjoy a rewarding career that has fulfilled many thousands of individuals. The rest of this book will survey the field and give you a sense of what public relations people do and where the opportunities lie.

CHAPTER 1

DEFINING PUBLIC RELATIONS AS A CAREER FIELD

Because a good public relations effort is applicable to so many aspects of everyday life, it is nearly impossible to arrive at an all-encompassing definition. This is further complicated by the fact that public relations, as it has grown in importance over the past few years, has also become more complex and diverse.

The Public Relations Society of America says: "Public relations helps an organization and its publics adapt mutually to each other. Often, it is a term used to describe both a way of looking at an organization's performance and a program of activities." Public relations efforts not only communicate a company or organization's story to the world; they also can help shape the organization itself.

The ultimate quality evaluation for any public relations campaign is the final performance. Though the information conveyed through public relations is crucial, the final judge of a campaign's effectiveness is what that distribution of information helps to achieve. Public relations is goal-oriented, and the final test is whether it achieves what it sets out to do.

As public relations specialists, we must constantly bear in mind that we communicate our messages to multiple and diverse publics. However, nothing today is carried out in an information vacuum, and we must assume that at any given time, the world is watching us and listening to what we say.

The messages we communicate must have the good of a society in mind, and that includes promoting products and causes. Public relations can be a force for good—a persuasive force. As such it has to be employed in the open, with public scrutiny. Public relations requires a degree of acceptance. It's one part of the job to communicate well—the other is to influence the audience to accept the messages and respond according to your design.

COMPARISON TO THE FIELD OF ADVERTISING

Public relations is often compared with advertising, and the two disciplines have many similarities. Both are persuasive and communicate through print and broadcast media. Both often strive toward the same goal or promote the same product or service. People who enter the two fields are commonly creative, full of energy, and stimulated by responsibility.

Both public relations and advertising are at their best when they work side by side. Most of advertising's messages are communicated through paid media. And in advertising, unlike public relations, where material appears at an editor's discretion, the agency has control of what appears in that space. It also tries to use variations on the same theme in each advertisement. Well-known themes repeated over and over include Nike's "Just Do It," the American Dairy Council's "Got Milk?," and AT&T's "Reach Out & Touch Someone." The public relations practitioner then employs these themes, expands on them, and adds others.

THE MARKETING ASPECT

The uses of the themes stem from the marketing function. Especially during a recession, the public relations professional must be more involved in marketing than ever—helping the client's cause or improving the client's profits. During inflationary periods, the client can buy considerably less advertising for his or her money than during good economic times, thus allowing a greater relative impact to be made by public relations.

In marketing terms, there is much more to the public relations function than "pushing a product." The economic impacts of our society have changed buying habits drastically, and the public relations person must help interpret why her or his company's product or service is a good buy.

To be an effective aid to marketing, the public relations craftsperson must know as much about the whole marketing process as the marketing manager; this process includes distribution, dealership, cooperative advertising, and warranties.

Public relations professionals must never lose sight of the fact that a major part of their mission is to persuade people, and this persuasion is not limited to clients. People make up diverse publics. The true test of public relations is its ability, through the expertise and capabilities of those who practice it, to market client's products to these myriad groups of people.

REACHING A DIVERSE PUBLIC

In order to reach, or "sell," these various groups, the public relations specialist must first identify them, ascertain what they do and how they fit in, and, above all, determine how best to influence them. Success in these areas is what expert marketing is all about.

A good public relations marketing effort is a preconditioning force that alerts customers to new products, new uses of products, and new ideas in the marketplace.

Hard-hitting, straight product publicity is one of the oldest functions of the public relations expert. As the professional practices the craft, he or she should not leave this vital function by the wayside to cope with only what challenges his or her intellect the most. Without publicity, which is the heart of marketing, clients will sell too few products, and when their cash registers don't ring, neither will those of the great corporate public relations departments and public relations firms.

Public relations serves marketing and sales. Sometimes it operates on its own, when there is no advertising campaign. But at its best, public relations is part of a combination punch.

MEDIA RELATIONS

A first-class public relations advisor will fight the trend of many insecure companies to retreat from the press. In doing so the public relations specialist improves the position of the client and the client's product. It is absolutely necessary to keep lines of communication between a client and the press open at all times.

As public relations experts, we must convince our clients that sometimes the press must report bad news, even if, temporarily, it may not present the client in the most favorable light. After all, it is a two-way street. We can't go back to the press with all the good news if we're not ready to inform them candidly about the bad.

It is the public relations person's job to serve as a bridge, a liaison, between the client and the press attempting to persuade the client to change her or his mind. We must make the client recognize what news really is, because often the person has no idea.

The best public relations firm in the world cannot help keep a company out of the newspapers. If it has a public profile at all, the firm must realize that it has a certain accountability to the public, including the media. A public relations firm can help by counterbalancing a bad image, which may occur from time to time.

Many corporations have well-trained, sophisticated, and competent public relations departments within their own boundaries, but they still seek the expertise of other outside firms. Why? There are as many valid answers as there are companies. Each has its own reason. On many occasions, the client seeks external help without really knowing exactly why. If there is a problem, the client may not realize the full extent of it.

Public relations firms represent corporations that want to examine themselves more closely to see if they want to present different images of themselves to their publics—to be seen in better or more positive light than that in which they believe they are currently being viewed.

A firm may hire a public relations specialist to help it avoid problems. Often, the public relations firm will put management through a host of questions and answers, discussing subjects the public and the media may ask about. When a corporation hires a public relations firm, it wants the communications expert to make sure that the firm stays out of trouble with the television stations and newspapers and other media. Candid feedback to the client, early in the game, can be bitter medicine, but it goes a long way toward avoiding eventual pitfalls.

Once problem areas are discussed up front between the public relations specialist and the client, the task is to persuade the media to cast the client in the desired perspective. Given the overwhelming abundance of news—international, national, state, and local—that bombards the communications media every day, there is an extremely limited amount of material that makes the evening television show or the morning papers. Selectivity has become the byword of the people who decide what makes news and what doesn't. Consequently, any corporation that wants to get its message across, using the airwaves, the Internet, or newspapers and magazines, must mold its messages in such a way that the decision makers choose it to be publicized.

DEVELOPMENT OF THE
PUBLIC RELATIONS INDUSTRY

Through growth in both clientele and sophistication, public relations companies are able to anticipate and deal with any press-related contingency that may arise. When public relations began as a profession, specialists dealt essentially with publicity, which was used as a device for marketing, whether it was for themselves or for a product. They scattered their message like buckshot without worrying a great deal about how they were perceived.

Then, as a number of companies went to the public for funds, public relations firms went into the disclosure and corporate image phase. Suddenly, for example, as in Washington law firms, one had to know how to deal with the government agencies, the Securities and Exchange Commission (SEC), financial analysts, and stockholders. It was a process of looking to see how the corporation was perceived by the public.

The third phase was the age of corporate responsibility. It came in the 1960s and 1970s when consumer advocate Ralph Nader touched off an outcry from individual consumers.

In public relations today, many of the outstanding practitioners of the art are "generalists." They range from discipline to discipline in a day's work. However, the strong economy of the 1990s increased the demand for technology, health care, and financial communications experts. Financial communications specialists in particular rise and fall with the Dow Jones. Many public relations veterans decry the growing demand for specialization.

THE PR PERSON TODAY

The public relations expert in the 2000s must be a businessperson first. Without a thorough knowledge of how to perform successfully in business, the practitioner not only will fail to sustain his or her own business but will also be unable to understand the needs and goals of the client.

Especially in today's exceedingly complex world, it is inappropriate and shortsighted to view the public relations specialist's role simply as that of a celebrity's press agent whose job it is to get the client mentioned in somebody's column. That is a far cry from dealing with the varied and complex problems of today's corporation.

Today's professional public relations person must have skills in many facets of life. Life has become so complex that problems are no longer easily placed in separate compartments to be dealt with by individual specialists. This does not mean that in understanding aspects of contemporary psychology, the public relations specialist intends to hang out a shingle as a consulting psychologist. However, he or she must be able to help both clients and the general public to better decipher the great amounts of information that is made public every day.

Satellite transmission, on-line data, the Internet, computers, and video cassettes are primary examples of revolutionary advances in communications that the public relations expert, his or her client, and much of the public must understand. Because new technologies can deliver information to several continents instantly, a public relations expert must have an understanding that the message will be received differently in San Antonio, Texas, and Sapporo, Japan. One needs only think of cross-cultural advertising campaign blunders to be sobered in the face of growing multiculturalism.

With the increasingly older American population, coupled with more leisure time for most adults, the public relations expert must, wearing his or her sociologist's hat, help people understand and deal with changes in their lives.

The permutations associated with one's choices in information outlets are already mind-boggling. Through the use of ever smaller and faster technology we are becoming more and more hooked in to information sources: Cell phones, E-mail, Palm Pilots, voice-activated computers in automobiles, and "smart" houses all can supply messages each moment to the public.

With today's miraculous communication advances come complicated choices that all of us must make. Consequently, the well-trained, hard-working, and skillful public relations specialist should have virtually limitless opportunities in the new century.

CHAPTER 2

HISTORICAL OVERVIEW OF PUBLIC RELATIONS

THE ROOTS OF THE PROFESSION

Today, with so many Americans working in some aspect of public relations, it seems hard to imagine that for centuries it existed as a "calling." Ancient civilizations understood the importance of good public relations techniques. With today's communications techniques, the art is very different, yet there are similarities. In ancient times, as today, public relations was used for one reason: to communicate. The early Greeks and Romans engaged in public relations in order to spread their message to as many people as possible. And disseminating information then was not as easy as it is with today's electronic communications.

Some form of public relations existed prior to the flourishing of the Roman and Greek civilizations. Priests in ancient Egypt excelled in influencing public opinion, persuading the general public to act, for the most part, as the priests desired. The priests used their power to various ends: to enhance (or to ruin) the current ruler's reputation, to guarantee that the art and literature of the day depicted the world according to their vision, and to ensure their own continued favor in the eyes of the people.

Elsewhere, in earlier times, public opinion focused entirely on the rulers, who used basic public relations tools to mold followers. The invention of writing significantly altered the molding of public opinion. For example, the literary legacy of ancient Assyria, Babylon, and Persia, preserved by means of elaborate scrolls and drawings, invariably portrays extremely brave and accomplished rulers. Of course, such impressions were most often molded directly by the monarchs themselves. The rulers thus ensured that public opinion would reflect what they wanted it to—not just during their lifetimes, but for all of history.

During the major period of growth in Greek civilization, priests played a less significant role in molding public opinion than they had earlier. Public opinion became more influenced by nonreligious or secular forces. There was a distinct separation of church and state. Therefore, government leaders, in contrast to church heads, independently assumed a role that they had previously shared, for the most part, with the religious hierarchy. These government leaders became very interested in public opinion, and not unlike heads of state in subsequent civilizations, they used public relations skills to influence what citizens thought. That was especially true in molding a favorable image of the leaders' accomplishments.

Relatively speaking, the Greek citizens in this era were encouraged to form and express their own opinions. Even though the leaders did attempt to present the most favorable image of themselves, they were not absolute dictators who insisted upon a nation of citizens who offered only constant praise concerning the governing bodies. At the same time, leaders did encourage the people to maintain a unified state spirit. This was based upon certain ideals that were considered necessary to run a productive and successful state. Leaders began to "take the pulse of the population" by conducting interviews; in effect, these represented examples of the earliest public opinion surveys. As the Greek city-states grew, so did the importance of public opinion, and the leaders used public relations methods to communicate with the general population.

The Roman Empire also emphasized public opinion, and its leaders made liberal use of public relations. Some of the great works of history were reflections of public opinion during the period. The history recorded by Julius Caesar and the great oratory of Cicero illustrate with primary examples how public opinion was formed. Written records and oratory often were used to direct the citizens toward a particular way of thinking. These were early methods of public relations that have endured throughout the centuries.

PROPAGANDA AND PUBLIC RELATIONS

In discussing the history of public relations, the word *propaganda* also must be noted. The word has changed in meaning since its inception during the seventeenth century.

Propaganda today can mean something negative, and it is not easy to define. However, according to the Institute for Propaganda Analysis, propaganda is an opinion offered by one or more persons that is designed to influence others' actions or opinions while referring to goals or ends that have already been determined.

This function of influencing others toward a predetermined end should not of itself be thought of as something negative. In fact, as H. Frazier Moore, University of Georgia journalism professor, has pointed out:

> In its broadest sense, propaganda is honest and forthright communication intended to advance a cause through enlightenment, persuasion, or a dedicated sense of mission. It is currently employed by religious, charitable, political, and social service institutions to influence the thoughts and actions of others for their best interests. In this sense, propaganda is legitimate persuasion.

But, as Frederick E. Lumley observed more than fifty years ago, many totalitarian governments throughout the world have used propaganda to further their own devious and harmful regimes. These dictatorships have twisted facts and presented false and inflammatory information: "Propaganda of every kind awakens passion by confusing the issues; it makes the insignificant seem weighty; it makes the important seem trifling; it keeps the channels of communication full of exciting stuff; it keeps people battling in a fog."

The major distinction between advertising, as we know it today, and propaganda is that the general public knows that the advertiser is attempting to persuade; the propagandist is more subtle. The advertiser tries to motivate the observer toward a certain course of action. In contrast, propaganda, as defined in the negative sense, contains a hidden or concealed goal or motivation. Most observers are not aware of the motivation—which is why propaganda can be bad. A perceptive and valid observation of public relations, and how it represents propaganda in the very best sense, was offered by Professor Moore:

> Public relations is sometimes referred to as propaganda. Since they are deliberately designed to influence public opinion, public relations programs may be considered as propaganda in the best sense of the word. Most public relations programs are honest and straightforward efforts to influence public opinion. However, as the word *propaganda* is commonly understood today, public relations is not propaganda; it is not a subversive activity that suppresses relevant facts, publishes false and misleading information, distorts the truth, and attempts to manipulate public opinion.

PUBLIC RELATIONS IN THE UNITED STATES

The history of public relations in the United States is as old as the country itself. The leaders of the American Revolution were outstanding public relations practitioners. They used written and oral methods of communications and persuasion extensively. The Declaration of Independence is an example of a written public relations technique. The revolution was not wholly accepted at first, and the early leaders absolutely had to master the art of persuasion. Among the early public relations artists were some of our best-known and most respected historical figures: Benjamin Franklin, Alexander Hamilton, John Jay, and Presidents Adams, Madison, and Jefferson. In addition to being an impressive political and legal document, the Declaration of Independence represented a stupendous public relations success.

In order to gain widespread acceptance of the Declaration, leading pamphleteers like Thomas Paine (*Common Sense*), James Madison, Alexander Hamilton, and John Jay (*The Federalist*) sold it and its ideals. American historian Phillip Davidson has pointed out that patriot Samuel Adams had no superior as a propagandist and that no one in the colonies either realized the importance of arousing public opinion better or took action as assiduously as he did.

Among these early masters of the skills of molding public opinion, a precursor of today's sophisticated public relations techniques, were Abigail Adams, Sarah Bache (Benjamin Franklin's daughter), Mercy Otis Warren, and Mary Katherine Goddard. Today, women have achieved more success in public relations than in almost any other profession and now outnumber men in the field.

PUBLIC OPINION IN THE 1800s AND EARLY 1900s

It was not until early in the nineteenth century that firm foundations were laid for public relations as we know it today. These bases were established just as the country saw a significant rise in the fortunes of the "great middle class." This improvement, in turn, was hastened by the fact that suddenly any male citizen could vote, regardless of whether he held property. Universal suffrage enabled the lower classes to take action toward issues that affected them. It also resulted in political and other leaders becoming more concerned with how to influence the masses.

Andrew Jackson, president of the United States from 1829 to 1837, was instrumental in devising techniques for communicating with and persuading the newly franchised voters. Mechanical innovations that would make the task easier to accomplish accompanied his thrust to influence the general public. The printing press, which had been operated by a hand lever beginning in 1813, gave way to the more complicated and efficient steam-driven one. By the time Jackson took office, the United States had more newspapers than any other country. Mass media began in 1833 with the *New York Sun,* which utilized the so-called penny press for the first time. Such changes contributed significantly to the growth of public persuasion—the art of practicing public relations.

When the Industrial Revolution took off in the first part of the nineteenth century, American industry promoted minimum interference by government and began to expand and prosper as never before. But the golden age of business prosperity produced many problems. Much of what was accomplished was couched in great secrecy. There was not always a great regard for how the growth of industry would be accepted by the public or how it would affect the general population.

Citizen groups began to protest the methods used by the emerging industrial giants. During the early part of the twentieth century, many people criticized the monopolies that gathered too much economic power in their own hands and shared little concern for people. Muckrakers like Ida Tarbell and Upton Sinclair, author of *The Jungle,* took on these giants, as did middle-class ordinary people who had decided that enough was enough.

Child labor abuses, unsafe working conditions, and ruthless business practices were widely condemned. The nation's largest businesses were stunned by the criticism, and corporations for the first time turned to public relations experts for help. The emerging giants of American industry had no choice but to enhance their relations with the public.

To help business react to muckrakers and social reform, and to help the government mobilize public opinion during the first world war, independent public relations specialists emerged. Some of the social problems and conditions they encountered are similar to those we deal with today. Labor unrest, periodic unemployment migrations from farms to cities, struggles against racial and sexual discrimination, competition from foreign products, and the loss of jobs due to factory relocation are difficulties yet to be overcome.

Innovations in communications in the form of radios and telephones were changing society then as drastically as home computers, E-mail, interactive television, and the Internet are now. Keeping in mind the question of scale, these periods saw change as monumental as in any other time in history.

THE ONSET OF BIG BUSINESS PUBLICITY

Ivy Lee: Industry Founder

With his publicity office in 1903, Ivy Lee became the first public relations counsel, although he evidently never used the term *public relations.* Lee became the first full-time practitioner of the art, which set the stage for what public relations has grown to be today. Originally called Parker & Lee, his firm represented the Pennsylvania Railroad and the anthracite coal operators. For the first time on a sizable scale, devoted to full-time public relations, Ivy Lee and his colleagues set forth a prototype for today's large, many-faceted public relations firms.

Lee used his and his colleagues' ingenuity and creativity to serve American business. That function remains the primary raison d'être of public relations firms and public relations departments today throughout the United States and the entire world.

Ivy Lee realized that he could not carry out programs on behalf of his client's business without having the direct support and cooperation of the client's top executive. Public relations, Lee discovered, did not operate in a vacuum. It was part of business, and each needed the other to be successful.

Ivy Lee also recognized that big business, as it was perceived early in the twentieth century, faced a sizable task in convincing ordinary people that it was out to improve their lives. Profit for profit's sake was often the only motto by which the early industrial leaders conducted their business affairs.

To Lee, the practice of business had to be changed, at least in terms of its image to the average American citizen. Big business had to become more human than it had been. Expansion, high finance, and ruthless competition were not easily comprehended by most Americans. The business of business, at its highest and most powerful levels, left a collective bad taste in the mouths of Americans.

Early public relations people like Lee set out to make the technical activities of business more understandable to everybody. He set out to make business more human. All businesses dealt in marketing something that somebody wanted. The product could be a tangible one like a candy bar or an automobile, or it could be the selling of a service. In either case, Ivy Lee emphasized the down-to-earth, common relationship between all Americans and the vast corporations expanding in the United States.

On behalf of the anthracite coal operators during a strike in the early 1900s, Lee set down his "Declaration of Principles," and insisted that newspapers publish them in order to inform the public fully. In his declaration, he spelled out clearly what his function as a public relations specialist was and how his role was carried out:

> This is not a secret press bureau. All our work is done in the open. We aim to supply news. This is not an advertising agency; if you think any of our matter ought properly to go to your business office, do not use it. Our matter is accurate. Further details on any subject treated will be supplied promptly, and any editor will be assisted most cheerfully in verifying any statement of

fact.... In brief, our plan is, frankly and openly, on behalf of business concerns and public institutions, to supply to the press and public of the United States prompt
and accurate information concerning subjects which it is
of value and interest to the public to know about.

Edward L. Bernays: Psychology and Public Relations

Edward L. Bernays—whose book, *Crystallizing Public
Opinion,* was published in 1923—had a profound influence
on the fledgling public relations field. In fact, Bernays's was
the first full-length book devoted to the workings of what
was to become contemporary public relations.

A man of stature in New York and Europe's literary world,
Edward Bernays firmly believed in the art of psychology
and in its application to public relations. He was a close relative of Sigmund Freud, the Viennese founder of psychoanalysis and one of the greatest thinkers of the twentieth
century. Bernays adapted the ideas of psychoanalysis and
applied them to public relations.

Bernays's belief in the interaction and feedback of individuals and their ideas was largely drawn from psychoanalysis. Nowhere are Bernays's ideas better described,
especially as they relate to this two-way process of psychology, than in his *Biography of an Idea: Memories of Public
Relations Counsel,* which was published in 1965.

My work with Liveright (a New York publisher)
represented a divide between what I had done—my
press-agentry, publicity, publicity direction—and
what I now attempted to do: counsel on public rela-

tions. This was no mere difference in nomenclature, no euphemistic changeover. It was a different activity, in approach and execution. From a one-way street of information and persuasion from client to public, it became a two-way street, with the element of adjustment added to the other two elements. Counsel on public relations was based on dealing with interaction between client and public.

Later, Edward Bernays taught the first public relations course at New York University; that, too, was a landmark in a profession that now is taught on many university campuses.

Not only did Edward Bernays play one of the key roles in the development of modern public relations, he also correctly predicted that during the last forty years of the twentieth century it would became a major field in American business and communications. Before Edward Bernays, there was no term *public relations* in our vocabulary. Today, it is hard to imagine the language without it, and the number of jobs in the area of public relations has increased significantly.

EXPECTED GROWTH OF THE FIELD

As the nature of doing business in the twenty-first century increases in complexity, the need for skilled communicators is bound also to increase. The Federal Bureau of Labor Statistics expects marketing, advertising, and public relations management positions to increase faster than average for all occupations through the year 2005. Global competition requires bigger and better responses from public relations and marketing specialists.

There are a number of reasons public relations will likely continue to be seen as a key aspect of corporate success. To paraphrase Elaine Goldman in an article for *The Public Relations Strategist* in 1998, these are the main considerations:

1. The increase in coverage of the economy and business in everyday media is teaching top executives the value of good media relations.
2. Leaders see the need for better communications inside a company to keep today's somewhat jaded employees on the team and on the same page.
3. There is a need to be able to manage communications in a global economy that spans continents and languages.
4. The growth of the Internet and "intranets" have caused a shifting of focus from a merely technical orientation to more of a content orientation.
5. The mounting chaos of communication clutter causes people to shut out the constant background buzz, which puts a premium on highly targeted efforts that resonate with sharply defined audiences.

Ms. Goldman is the president of The Goldman Group, Inc., a New York executive recruiting and management consulting company, and a former public affairs executive, professor of broadcast journalism, and TV and newspaper reporter. Her words ring very true now in the early years of the twenty-first century. Edward Bernays would probably not be surprised that public relations is a much-used term and a key aspect of today's economy.

CHAPTER 3

PUBLIC RELATIONS IS EVERYWHERE

POLITICS

Public relations plays a key role in everyday life. Look around and you will realize that the use of public relations is very extensive. For example, when a United States congressional member mails her or his newsletter each month to constituents, this is practicing public relations. How? Through the newsletter, the senator or representative gains valuable exposure. Constituents notice not only the person's name, but also his or her photograph. The newsletter also describes legislative accomplishments, emphasizing activities that the congressperson believes will be important to the potential voters in the congressional district.

By emphasizing the positive, in terms of her or his legislative efforts, that member of Congress is practicing public relations. That person is enhancing her or his reputation and image in the public's eye. And that means, most of all, that he or she is projecting a positive or favorable image to those eligible to vote the next time that he or she runs for office.

In addition to United States senators and congresspersons, virtually every segment of government uses public relations. In fact, its use on the state or local level is not essentially different from the way in which it is used nationally. For example, when a state legislator from southern Illinois introduces legislation to benefit the coal industry, he or she announces it to constituents, not unlike the way a certain senator from Nebraska let the entire state know what he or she had accomplished toward raising milk price supports.

Local public officials also distribute press releases, position papers, and arrange television appearances in order to get their messages across.

NEWSPAPERS

There are many other examples of public relations in everyday life. Once a week, in major newspapers, food sections run feature stories on a wide range of topics. For example, one may read a piece on the health hazards of salt or the nutritional value of 2 percent milk. Although both are feature stories, they have significant educational components and serve as public relations vehicles.

Such stories impart health information that is directly beneficial to the reader or consumer. By conveying this knowledge to hundreds of thousands of readers, a newspaper may shower invaluable rewards on companies and industries mentioned in the articles. After reading the pieces, the reader concludes, consciously or unconsciously, that the company mentioned in the article has performed a good deed, thus enhancing its image.

TELEVISION

No better example of the use of public relations exists than a guest appearance on a television talk show. With more than sixty-five thousand books being published each year in the United States, editors, literary agents, and publishers compete vigorously to book their authors to appear on such shows. Local programs are desirable, but national ones—especially *Larry King Live, The Tonight Show,* and *The Today Show*—are coveted most, as are the David Letterman and Oprah Winfrey shows, both of which have enormous audiences. In addition, literally dozens of other talk shows litter the airwaves, as do the new phenomena, "infomercials"—shows that look like shows but are actually commercials.

Why? With an audience of millions of people, an appearance on such a show creates huge numbers of potential buyers. Book sales often take off noticeably after a successful talk show appearance. But once an author discusses her or his book on one of these shows, even if only for a minute or two, he or she has piqued the interest of many, many listeners.

SOCIAL ACTIVIST CONCERNS

Virtually every organization in the country uses some form of public relations. Community activists, proponents of nearly every social cause, virtually every level of government, and large corporations all try to convey their messages through public relations.

For example, when one of Ralph Nader's consumer groups decides to state its views for or against a product, it does so through a well-orchestrated public relations campaign. It wastes no time telling the major news media about its point of view. Above all, this group wants to get its message across to a large number of people, and the best way to do that is to attract the attention of large-circulation newspapers and television stations in the nation's largest cities. And often, all it takes to do this is a simple, well-written, factually correct press release.

When certain groups utilize public relations techniques, they are initiating the dissemination of a certain point of view. For example, when the citizens' lobby Common Cause wants its thousands of members to lobby senators and congresspersons to vote for a certain piece of legislation, they do not wait for opposite viewpoints to be expressed in order to react. Instead, Common Cause seizes the initiative and starts the lobbying process. Other powerful lobbying forces include the National Rifle Association and the American Association of Retired Persons.

Primarily armed with a highly educated membership, grassroots groups attempt to influence members of Congress by calling and writing to them. This is what public relations is all about—individuals or groups putting forth their message in order to influence others.

Other citizen groups initiate public relations activities, using methods similar to those of large corporations. To influence legislation or to urge a new national thrust, the NAACP, the labor unions, and the National Organization for Women (NOW) select specific public relations tools.

EDUCATION

Schools, both public and private, depend on public relations to promote their educational activities. For example, private schools and colleges, to make the case for their higher fees, print and distribute sophisticated brochures for prospective students, emphasizing the advantages they offer. Sometimes the school's staff designs, writes, and prints these pamphlets, but often, to ensure professionalism, schools hire outside experts to help with their mission.

On a more basic level, everyday school fund-raising is public relations. Spring fairs and fall festivals organized by parents involve much time in getting their message across. Time-consuming posting of leaflets on telephone poles around the neighborhoods, coupled with radio and television messages, supplement the efforts of the students who, with good intentions, don't always carry news to those who should receive it.

ENTERTAINMENT

No segment of society is more public relations-conscious than the entertainment industry. Movies, television, and theater rely on public relations as their lifeblood to create a larger-than-life image. Of course, public relations can't sell a bad television program, movie, or Broadway play, but it can help. And it can aid in appealing to a larger number of viewers. Public relations gets people talking about the production's reputation, and word of mouth draws more customers. Nevertheless, when movies cost millions of dollars, reliance on word of mouth to create crowds at the box office is not sufficient to guarantee the film's success.

In the movie industry, no matter how financially successful a movie turns out to be, and regardless of the popularity of its leading actors, nothing is taken for granted in terms of guaranteeing maximum public relations between the industry and the general moviegoing public.

Have you ever asked yourself how local film critics receive excerpts from the best parts of movies, neatly prepared on videotape? And how do ordinary people hear about films? In today's youth-oriented film industry, inordinately large numbers of young people make up the viewing audience. Efforts to sell the movies are directed specifically at them—ticket promotions on radio stations and stars' appearances on *Saturday Night Live* are part of this effort.

One of the world's greatest movie promotion events is the Academy Awards. With the glamour, the stars, the suspense, and the legions of movie fans, it might seem that public attention is virtually guaranteed. Yet to make sure that millions of people see a well-run, first-class performance, conveying a true, positively perceived impression, a sophisticated public relations campaign begins well in advance of the Academy Awards ceremony night. And on Oscar night itself, press coverage is organized to reach the waiting world with maximum efficiency.

SPORTS

Sports is also a form of entertainment. Newspapers, magazines, and television devote almost as much space to sports as to national politics. Yet sports teams are private businesses, managed for their owners' profit. This circumstance involves public relations at a high level—justifying athletes' high salaries, encouraging attendance for winning and losing teams, arranging appearances for players to personalize the team's public image, and creating special events (like Boy Scout nights, left-handed-people days, and so forth) to keep interest alive when the play on the field is dull.

Public relations is used in high school sports, too. By posting an announcement about a basketball game between two local schools, ordinary citizens are practicing public relations at a very basic level.

Through these examples, we have seen that the average American, as well as large government, movie, and sports organizations, can enjoy highly sophisticated public relations skills. Every day we come in contact with some form of public relations, and we are not often aware of it.

Through these examples, showing how the "person next door" has direct access to public relations activities, we trust you'll agree public relations is available to everyone, not only to large government or corporate institutions.

HEALTH CARE

This has been a growth industry, educating people about wellness, their health, and improved lifestyles. The introduction of pharmaceutical products is one of the vibrant areas of the field. Following is a recap of how the field looks to an expert.

The New Health Care Playing Field
by Richard E. Rotman[*]

This is a new era for the health care communications industry, in which change is so rapid that many are not certain of what the result will be. The third-party payers, drug benefits managers, stakeholder groups, and patients who influence market access have all but obliterated the comfortable old triad of patient-doctor-pharmacist. The only certainty is change (yet what is ahead is so uncertain!).

The reasons for this change are numerous, but primarily, there appears to be worldwide consensus—reached long ago in Canada—that controlling health care costs is in the interests of the state, and that corporations can influence this large cost item and employees can benefit. This is a seismic change

---

[*]Richard Rotman is a public relations professional with experience in the health care industry.

for all communications professionals. It makes health care communications in part a function of government relations. In addition, in the United States, the world's largest pharmaceutical market, President and Mrs. Clinton's initiative to place health care squarely on the public agenda may have lost the battle but won the war. Although it failed as legislation in 1994, it produced consensus that something is wrong and has to be fixed, a characteristic American motivation for new laws.

In addition, there have been huge corporate mergers and acquisitions in the health care field, which also influence future opportunities for communicators. Merck, the perennial market leader, signaled the nature of the new era so dramatically when it acquired Medco, a managed-care company. Then Eli Lilly purchased PDS, a pharmacy benefit company, Hoffman-La Roche bought Syntex, SmithKline purchased Diversified, and Kodak sold Sterling Drugs. Almost every leading firm in the field is considering its own future organization and how it will meet the new challenges.

Health care leaders may be thinking globally, but they are also looking ahead to consider the need for local coalitions, partnerships, temporary industry groups, and cross-industry organizations for the years ahead. Working together with governments, stakeholder groups, hospitals, third-party payers, and other players in the same product sector was not standard practice in the past—but it is now. Communicators skilled in arranging these coalitions, partnerships, and working groups will thrive in this environment.

To understand the new health care playing field, here is a short guide:

1. Key stakeholder groups—disease- and condition-related foundations and charities—find themselves in very strong positions. If they do not favor a new medication, its chances of market acceptance are dimmed. These groups include: patient and disease information groups and intergroup coalitions, and state and local as well as national organizations.

The strength of these groups reflects the new patient-centered medical model. Patients often ask for particular medications, which doctors feel pressured to prescribe or risk losing patients. The top-down model of the doctor telling the patient what he or she should take is fading away rapidly, which explains the dramatic increase in pharmaceutical advertising directed at consumers.

2. Physicians are unquestionably still the most important influencers, but reaching and influencing them is one of the most difficult challenges in the communications industry. There will be many new developments in electronic communications with physicians and their pharmacist counterparts. Today, the information highway provides on-line access and provides for smooth transfer of patient records. However, few physicians have embraced the computer age, and most patients still prefer to visit a doctor in person.

Future health care communicators should note that focusing on building relationships with such groups as physicians and their many specialties, pharmacists, regulators, and third-party payers, whether they are governments or insurance organizations, is far more important than widespread media coverage. More precise communications targeting is our ultimate goal.

Many of these individuals, interestingly, are women. Because of the qualities of caring and empathy, women are moving quickly into positions of leadership in health care, much as they already have in communications.

3. Alternate pharmaceutical distribution systems, such as mail order, are growing and will provide employment opportunities. This is probably one of the more significant developments challenging the relationship with the community-based pharmacists, and only massive investments in customer service, counseling, and information in drugstores will slow this particular aspect of change. Leading pharmacy chains toward a more service-oriented attitude will keep numerous young communicators busy in the future.

4. Managed care, or corporate control of health care costs, is, of course, the most prominent development in the United States. Even though the system is different in Canada, it still will seriously impact that country. Large companies, benefits consultants, and union drug plans stand at the center of this new health care landscape and influence every cost from drug company to physician to consumer.

All of the above appears to indicate industry volatility, and certainly in some sectors downsizing is happening. But there are also tremendous growth possibilities. Where, then, are the employment and career growth opportunities in the developments just described?

Science graduates certainly have an advantage in dealing with their counterparts in pharmaceutical companies and hospitals. But humanities-oriented students also should seriously consider the field. Health care will always be a growth field in need of individuals to explain scientific findings and terms to a general audience. And that is where the future of health care public relations lies. It is no different from any other technical field except that the rewards of providing better health can be significant to the individual practitioner.

The opportunities are also in change. Look for change and watch in which direction it is taking place, especially in health care. Think in terms of education and change of behavior and habit, rather than in communication of an issue, viewpoint, or product. Embrace change, and head in its direction.

In change there is opportunity—both for those already in the field and those seeking to enter or sell a product or service to it. Watching where the change is taking the industry is absorbing and is sometimes a roller-coaster ride for those inside attempting to manage it. But the rewards also can be great, if one can look ahead.

CHAPTER 4

WHY THE PUBLIC RELATIONS FIELD KEEPS EXPANDING

At no time in our nation's history has there been more interest in the population's opinion. Improved technology makes it easier to determine what people believe on almost any issue, and use of research and opinion polls undoubtedly will become even more widespread. Consequently, the need for public relations experts, who play a major role in molding public opinion, has never been greater. In fact, many larger PR firms are now either linked with or operate research companies.

OPINION POLLS

The opinions of the public are sought for many reasons. American businesses constantly ask questions, through telephone polls or written questionnaires, to find out the tastes and preferences of American consumers. They also poll employees to check the level of support for their policies. Car manufacturers, cosmetic makers, and cereal producers spend millions of dollars each year trying to find out what Americans prefer.

There are many full-time, large companies that conduct these polls under contract to corporations, politicians, government agencies, and trade associations that are extremely interested in specific answers to scientifically developed questions. In addition to Harris, Gallup, and Roper organizations, which are well known because of their longtime, extensive political pools, there are many other polling organizations, employing thousands of people. A new research area involves message testing for public relations purposes. President Reagan's handlers first employed this technique to determine the highest audience approval. Now pioneers at this technique, such as Rowan & Biewitt, of Washington, DC, test audience reaction to negative television coverage, among many other topics, to determine the best audience reaction to an issue.

Opinion surveys help public relations practitioners educate a wide segment of the American people about the benefits of any given product. Providing surveys to America's major corporations is a large part of the function of the nation's foremost public relations firms and their counterparts in corporate public relations departments.

Educating the public involves projecting a positive, wholesome image of the represented company to the different publics it is trying to reach. Public relations is image building: It is making sure that a company is seen in the best possible light by those who see its advertisements on television or read them in magazines and newspapers. This cannot be overemphasized.

Now more than ever, people in all segments of the general public have a great deal of power.

AN EDUCATED POPULACE

The public relations expert, as well as the producer of the product, must never underestimate the intelligence of the prospective consumer and should never talk or write down to her or him. With ever larger percentages of Americans attending college and graduating from high school, people have become too well informed to be significantly led astray.

Although watching television for hours at a time is regarded by many people as a waste of time, it is a proven method for receiving a large volume of information. Consequently, presenters of that huge dose of information must not, in any way, try to dupe the millions of people who watch their television sets from forty to sixty hours each week. It simply won't work. People are becoming much more sophisticated and cynical.

Along with the increased educational level of millions of Americans comes instantaneous radio, television, and Internet communication. Through satellites, television allows people anywhere in the United States to see a war overseas or a World Cup soccer match from anywhere in the world as they occur. We only have to turn on our television sets to view history in progress.

If we happen to be away from our sets when an event occurs, we can set our VCRs and have instant replay at our convenience. Anyone interested in a breaking story can log on at work or home and follow it closely. The Internet and on-line services automatically clip stories of interest for subscribers.

With the advent of such sophisticated communication processes, and with the promise of yet unknown new technology, an equally skilled and sophisticated public relations practitioner has already become a necessity. A broadly experienced public relations expert is often needed to instruct a client about possible pitfalls—problems that the firm should anticipate so that it knows how to react if and when they occur. Corporations—even those having a well-staffed in-house public relations division—constantly feel the need to go outside their firms to enlist the expertise of other public relations specialists. They utilize independent skills to deal with a wide assortment of public relations problems in conjunction with a broad range of products. They hire experts who can see the "big picture."

RELATING TO HOSTILE PUBLICS

It is one thing to report generally the existence of "value conflicts" between businesses and other groups in our society. It is another to report that a company's stockholders are accusing it of economic sin or that its employees are at the point of staging anti-exploitation walkouts. It is even more difficult to report that consumers have filed petitions with several federal and state agencies, and that the general public erroneously believes that corporations are "ripping off" the consumer to the tune of 28 percent net profit each year. It takes a tough skin to insist that these problems also be added to management's worries.

Even the middle class is getting restless! And that means the bulk of all of us, America's primary consumers. For this reason, the public relations expert will have to stay ahead of rapidly changing business and societal conditions. Public relations will still have to react to difficult situations, but above all, the new public relations industry will depend on skilled practitioners who anticipate trends. The public relations professional must be able to teach the client to comprehend that the world is in a drastic state of change and to cope with those changes.

At times, the public relations person must exhibit the fervor of an evangelist when competing for a client's attention. But the well-grounded client will have respect for the professional in the field who continues to point out that many of the client's problems are related to public relations and that creative and successful techniques are needed to solve them.

Keep in mind that the hallmarks of the public relations craft are communications and persuasion. Specialists must hone their understanding of the forces that change public attitudes, that change a group of cooperative employees into a surly mob, that change loyal customers into dissidents, and that change placid stockholders into irritated lobbyists.

CHAPTER 5

PUBLIC RELATIONS IN CANADA

Public relations, like television, arrived somewhat later in Canada than it did in the United States, but then it grew rapidly and became more technologically advanced because it did not have as much past history to overcome.

It's said that Canada is a caring country, and for that reason public relations, a caring profession, has taken root deeply. The social penalties in Canada for poor corporate citizenship or even elitism in providing health care are severe. Therefore, the idea of serving the people is taken very seriously.

Canada, of course, offers many public relations challenges, due to several prominent factors. Canada is larger geographically than the United States, but its population is smaller than California's. The great majority of its citizens live within one hundred miles of the U.S. border. There is, of course, a large French-speaking population in Quebec, and the country is officially bilingual, even though English is the dominant language. Canada is very regional, and different parts of the country do not have the same common feelings as do those in the United States. In fact, certain corners of the country appear to have more similarities with their U.S.

counterparts to the south; this holds true with British Columbia and Washington state and the Maritime provinces and New England.

THE CLOSE BOND BETWEEN CANADIAN AND AMERICAN PUBLIC RELATIONS

Few American communicators are aware how much Canada is a part of the U.S. communications grid. Despite a lively film industry, 97 percent of the films seen in Canada are Hollywood products. CNN and the superstations—Chicago's WGN, Boston's WSBK, New York's WOR, and Atlanta's TBS—are seen on most cable systems. Neighboring local stations are also part of the cable television grid; Toronto, for example, has a choice of its own stations and networks and also broadcasts from neighboring Buffalo and Rochester plus superstations. The *New York Times, U.S.A. Today,* and the *Wall Street Journal* are available daily in major cities. Many Canadian newspapers reprint stories from these publications as major parts of their news coverage. And Canadians are far more knowledgeable about U.S. politics and trends than Americans will ever be about developments to the north.

Canadians are extremely influential in the United States, yet few Americans are aware of this. In fact, the following cultural figures are Canadian: ABC's Peter Jennings; Blues Brother Dan Aykroyd; *Saturday Night* and *Wayne's World* producer Lorne Michaels; comic actor Martin Short; the *Terminator's* creator James Cameron; The Band's Robbie Robertson; David Letterman's sidekick Paul Shaffer; *Jeopardy's*

Alex Trebek; plus Wayne Gretzky and dozens of hockey players and the two-time World Series champion, the Toronto Blue Jays.

The North American Free Trade Act, plus many collaborations in film and television production, have caused the United States and Canada to grow closer. Even so, it is a mistake to think that one can cover Canada by communicating only through the U.S. national media. Some penetration does occur that way, but Canadian media overwhelmingly try to find the Canadian angle or the Canadian expert in any news coverage. Many American experts are used in news conferences, especially in the health care field, but more often than not journalists will quote the Canadian spokesperson first, no matter how eminent the visiting American may be. The reverse also would be true at an American news conference.

SPECIFIC PUBLIC RELATIONS
CHALLENGES IN CANADA

French is a special demand of working in Canadian public relations. National announcements usually require two news conferences—one in English-speaking Toronto, the country's communications center, and one in French-speaking Montreal. That means that translation of news materials and spokespeople in Montreal who can handle French and English are required. Very few English-speaking Canadians are in fact bilingual. People of French origin—called Francophones— comprise the majority of those who can handle both languages skillfully. Bilingualism adds to the expense both of government and of the communications professions.

Although Quebec has made many political moves to separate from the rest of Canada, it remains deeply tied to the nation at least economically and politically. That being said it is important to note that Quebec continues to assert control over its own destiny in a fashion that is unknown and somewhat impossible in the United States (as is the issue of secession, long ago settled in the Civil War).

Regionalism also adds to the expense of any public relations effort. Those in western Canada wish to know how announcements pertain to their special interests, and those in Atlantic Canada, the country's fifth time zone, are concerned with their region, too. (There are actually five and a half time zones; Newfoundland's time is one half hour ahead of the rest of the country.) There is far more use of regional spokespeople representing their province's interest than an individual representing a large state or region. The ten provinces—Canada's equivalent of a state—are far more powerful than any American state. Provinces operate Canada's health care system, run hospitals and universities, collect a large share of income taxes, and share news coverage equally with the federal government. Canada's national base is Ottawa, Ontario, the only province to have two capitals (and not a federal district, as occurs in Washington, DC, or Mexico City).

All of the big U.S. counseling firms have set up offices in Canada, and there are also large Canadian independent firms. The actual day-to-day workings of the profession are very similar to the typical practitioner's U.S. experience. Because print media still occupy a larger share of public consciousness and literacy is more highly valued, Canadians still tend to read more than their American cousins. However, national television networks—Much Music and Newsworld are clones of MTV and CNN—have added national specialized news to more regional offerings.

Canada also considers itself multicultural rather than a melting pot or even a multiracial society like that in the United States. There is an effort to preserve not only Native culture but also the languages and values of the many European, Slavic, and Asian cultures that have flocked to this large, somewhat unpopulated country. There are special opportunities for communicators who understand Asian cultures, as Canada allowed many people from Hong Kong to emigrate in advance of the Chinese takeover in 1997. Huge Chinese groups exist in Toronto and Vancouver, and they have added to an interesting population mix and created special linguistic and cultural communications challenges.

Canada's cities are dynamic and largely clean and safe, so if an opportunity arises to work there, you may want to seriously consider it. Canada will broaden your sense of the United States and its self-proclaimed global leadership, not to mention the differences inherent in a bilingual society with a parliamentary government that is still connected to England's monarchy.

CHAPTER 6

THE PUBLIC RELATIONS PROFESSIONAL

There has never before been as wide a variety of areas in which one can play a key role as in the area of public relations.

Here are just some of the different fields in which a properly trained professional can work as a public relations specialist: public affairs, community relations, public information, media relations, public opinion, government relations, political campaigns, consumer affairs, commercial business, and research and statistics.

CHARACTERISTICS OF PUBLIC RELATIONS AS A PROFESSION

Before looking closer at these specific areas, let's first examine some characteristics of the profession. As an industry, public relations did not begin to grow appreciably until after World War II. Prior to that, for the most part, people entering the field did not necessarily receive any specific education or training. Colleges and universities offered few, if any, courses in the field. And it was unheard of to receive a degree or major in public relations. However, there was one great training ground for many public relations specialists: newspapers.

Let's get personal for a moment.

Morris Rotman, Young Journalist

I was a student at Wright Junior College and a part-time employee at a local Chicago shoe store. A year earlier, I had nervously carried my writing samples to Leo Lerner of the Lerner newspapers. I had been editor of the Tuley High School *Review* newspaper and editor of Wright's literary magazine.

One lucky day, Leo Lerner called and asked if I would be interested in a two-week, vacation-fill-in job on the *Lincoln-Belmont Booster,* the only paper in what was later to become the fifty-paper Lerner chain.

"Would I!" I exclaimed. Actually, I was probably too excited to reply coherently. The two-week assignment started a career in journalism and subsequently in public relations. I am extremely proud of my thirty-six years building Harshe-Rotman & Druck, Inc., and then merging to form Ruder, Finn & Rotman, which came into being on January 1, 1982.

Fortunately, those two weeks in journalism led first to a summer job and then later to a full-time job on a new Lerner paper. I was so proud being a professional newspaper reporter. Also, the pay was a strong inducement. My formal education would be finished at night.

Journalism offered me an invaluable education that prepared me very well for my subsequent career in public relations. Most of all, I learned how to communicate well. Of course, this was done in print. But before putting words on paper, I had to organize my thoughts in order to write well. And my pieces had to be persuasive. I have paid close attention to honing my skills of communication since then. Even now, after some success in my chosen field, I take nothing for granted. Each task is new and exciting. Each one is challenging. And on every project, I must apply the same basic skills of analysis, communication, and persuasion that I learned many years ago.

I must have been doing something right. I advanced to larger papers and briefly reported for the Chicago *Sun-Times*. My most important training came at The City News Bureau of Chicago, famed training ground for many outstanding journalists. I was a police reporter; I covered most beats, became a rewrite man, and was an assistant city editor by the time I left. Eventually, I entered the public relations field through the Community and War Fund of Metropolitan Chicago, where I served as publicity director.

Later, I joined the firm where I spent most of my career in public relations.

Journalism is still a fertile training ground for people who wish to become public relations professionals. Entry-level jobs pay a bit more than what I made when I started. Journalism still provides the same kind of excellent training that I received. Most of all, it teaches you to make sure that you communicate in a clear and precise fashion. And no public relations specialist can exist without the requisite skills in communication.

Today, many journalists move freely into the public relations field. Top journalists from the major daily newspapers become spokespeople for the highest government officials, and following government service, they either return to daily journalism or enter the public relations field. Some join the internal public relations departments of major corporations, while others join public relations firms.

When one decides that he or she wants to become a professional public relations practitioner, he or she no longer has to begin training on the job. Formal education begins at the college or university level.

PERSONAL REFLECTIONS

When I started in the public relations field, what we did essentially was obtain free publicity for our clients. The people or organizations that hired us wanted to get their share of press attention. It was our job to capture the editor's eye by using bright approaches that would make interesting reading. In my professional book, there were always two ways to get publicity: report it or create it.

We staged press conferences; arranged stunts and photo opportunities for the press; and sent out memos, telegrams, and other communications alerting the press to what we thought was a good story. In most cases, the press was receptive to a creative idea or a new piece of information that would make newspapers and programs lively and more interesting. We also provided access to stories the press couldn't easily get. Our people used their ingenuity in thinking up creative ways to alert members of the press and get them out for an event.

We spent a lot of time "planting" items in gossip columns. In the early days, a mention in Walter Winchell's nationally syndicated column appeared in more than two thousand newspapers. Winchell ran a column full of short items interspersed with three dots...I proudly told a client I got him into the column one day. He dismissed the achievement saying he wanted paragraphs, not sentences.

Being a press agent, still a proud calling despite the spreading umbrella of public relations, calls for ingenuity, personal contact with the press, and an ability to write catchy stories. Winchell had a "blackmail" system for press agents he favored. If you fed him several items where you were not commercially involved, he would favor the items you needed to get into his column.

Our associate in New York, Earle Ferris, ran a very successful news service wherein he supplied by wire anecdotal items about his broadcast performer clients. Every week hundreds of telegrams with funny little stories and witty sayings that were allegedly quoted by his clients went out to columnists. Most of his material was written by a nerdy-looking little guy who dropped off a stack of copy every Saturday without ever saying a word to anyone. He never spoke but once nodded to me. He was paid $200 a month for his output and his name was Woody Allen.

One day we were hired by a Chicago television performer to get his name in the papers. I suggested a daily television column, written by my client, to Lou Shainmark, managing editor of Chicago's *Herald American* newspaper. Shainmark rejected the idea, telling me that television stations would have to pay for any free space they got. Count the inches of coverage in today's newspapers and magazines! Shainmark was a great newspaper editor but he predicted wrong on that one.

Most successful publicity campaigns were built on a unique, new idea. John MacArthur, later famous for the MacArthur Foundation genius scholarships, hired us to publicize his fledgling insurance company. He had his own plane and I worked out a "Mercy Fleet" of other corporate planes in cooperation with the Red Cross to fly missions of mercy in emergencies. A newspaper agreed to sponsor the service and featured it on its front page. MacArthur became commander of the fleet and his picture appeared on the front page several columns wide announcing the idea. Incidentally, MacArthur, a tight-fisted iconoclast, must be spinning in his grave in realization how his trustees are giving away his money to geniuses, who don't have to account for it.

Our firm acquired dubious notoriety because of a press stunt that went wrong. We lost the account as a result. Our client, a dog food manufacturer, introduced a pure beef pellet for dogs, and the president of the company illustrated the quality of the product by popping a morsel in his mouth. One of our people thought of the idea of having the press in while the executive and a handsome dog had lunch together. Unfortunately, the cameras and commotion scared the dog and he wouldn't eat. Front page headline in a business journal read: "President Eats Dog Food But Dog Won't." Moral: never use children and animals in press stunts.

One of our best campaigns was for the National Restaurant Association, which asked us to develop a hospitality program for its members that would help foster cordial relations between customers and employees. The result was the "We're Glad You're Here" campaign, which was in use by NRA members for more than ten years. There were buttons, banners, counter tents, contests for employees, and other communications devices telling customers "We're Glad You're Here." Other industry groups bought the buttons and graphics for their industries, too. (We were appalled when we heard a funeral service group bought "We're Glad You're Here" buttons.)

I particularly was proud of the cross-promotional tie-in we worked out between our client, The National Bowling Council, and The American Cancer Society and Wheaties. The cereal company gave our client publicity on their millions of Wheaties boxes plus about a half-million dollars worth of advertising urging consumers to "Bowl Down Cancer." It was a successful three-way parlay for all concerned.

Quite by accident, I created a new industry association at one point in my career. A good friend, Syd Baren, decided to add a swimming pool to his suburban home near Chicago. He asked if I knew where he could get information about swimming pools from a centralized source. I could find none, which led me to call several swimming pool manufacturers, who affirmed my suspicion that there was need for an industry group. The next thing I knew, I had organized the National Swimming Pool Institute; written its by-laws with the help of my attorney; designed a logo for the new name;

and called a meeting of the new group of about 150 people at a downtown Chicago hotel.

As a former newspaperman, I was pleased when the *New York Times* retained us to explore why the paper, despite extraordinarily generous employment practices, suffered repeated labor unrest. One of the things we discovered was that the company didn't know how to communicate with its own employees. Despite hundreds of writers in the paper's employ, our people wrote the first internal publication for employees of the *Times.*

At another juncture in my career, our firm was hired by the Chicago *Sun-Times,* which suffered some serious losses in circulation, advertising, and public esteem in the wake of its acquisition by Rupert Murdoch. Subscribers fled in droves in anticipation of how Murdoch would change the paper for the worse, and the paper lost a lot of its upscale advertising. Many subscribers canceled their subscriptions when they saw the sleazy front-page headlines and stories that were part of the Murdoch journalistic style.

My adventures on that account, working directly with publisher Bob Page and business manager Don Piazza, deserve a full book. We staged a number of focus groups in various parts of Chicago and Frank Devine, then executive editor, allowed me to address the editorial board on what we had found out about subscribers' negative attitudes toward the new Murdoch-controlled *Sun-Times.* Page asked me to prevail upon them to tone down the vulgar journalistic approach, which so many people in our focus groups told us they were offended by. My pleas fell on deaf ears because they reported to Devine, who was a Murdoch disciple. Devine called the shots on the front-page treatment. Murdoch didn't quite understand that Chicagoans were a conservative lot and resented the purchase and cheapening of a Chicago institution.

Devine, a charming, witty, and erudite journalist originally from New Zealand, who functioned in adversarial opposition to publisher Page, became a good friend and listened to some of my ideas. But he called me the "devil's own disciple" because he knew Page had hired me, and I allegedly represented his viewpoints. Murdoch gave Devine and Page equal authority and they functioned in a constant state of disagreement with me acting as the ameliorating go-between. Later Page assembled enough financing to buy the paper but was himself forced out by the majority ownership group. When Page took over the paper, I handed him copy for a by-lined front-page editorial called "Publisher's Credo." It bore his name and he ran it two columns wide with modest corrections of my copy.

As our firm grew, we added people from the financial field to handle annual reports and financial news; experienced corporate public relations people to organize and execute campaigns consistent with the business objectives of corporations; home economists to develop campaigns for the food pages; and several other disciplines to carry out the specialized functions of a communications campaign. Along the line, we acquired a firm specializing in financial public relations. We also added a research department headed by a man with a doctorate in mass communications.

At one time, we added a design studio to work on symbols, corporate names, and to add professional design to most of the materials we turned out for our clients. We established a professional photographic studio to control the quality of the pictures we got for our publicity campaigns. We also started a full-service letter shop to handle mailing lists, reproduction of materials, and all kinds of printing assignments short of big and complicated brochures. We believed it was important to get quick service when we needed it. Also we wanted to protect confidential client mailing lists.

Our transition from a regional public relations firm to one with national scope occurred when we were hired by Hertz Rent-a-Car, our first major national client, to publicize their growing service. At that time, Hertz was owned by General Motors, and it was a big leap for us to have GM on our client list. When Hertz went public, we had to learn to handle financial and corporate communications.

One time, we went to see an editor of the *Saturday Evening Post* about a possible Hertz story. At first he declined to do it, saying "only kidnappers, stickup men, and philanderers rent cars." Ultimately we did get big features in the *Post, Readers Digest,* and almost every major national publication. Our publicity helped pave the way for public acceptance of car and truck rental as an everyday socially correct business and personal occurrence.

We made the leap into international public relations when our clients needed additional coverage in Europe, Canada, and ultimately throughout the world. We acquired part ownership of a firm in London. Our firm also acquired a U.S.-

based company that had a network of representatives in twenty-six countries, some of them one-person public relations shops but in other cases full-sized public relations firms like those in England, France, Germany, and Japan. A full-service public relations firm must have service available wherever its clients do business.

Part of my career was spent learning how to function as a public relations man in England, France, Germany, Spain, Italy, the Scandinavian countries, and Japan. I even took a basic Berlitz course in Japanese and was surprised to find out that the word in Japanese for public relations was "PR."

One of our most successful public relations campaigns was for Mattel, Inc., the toy maker. Mattel started out as a modest publicity account. As the company grew, so did we. We carried out special marketing, financial, corporate, and international programs for the company. At one time it represented a major portion of our California billings.

In order to better communicate with parents of Barbie doll owners, who were furious about all the television advertising urging their children to ask for new Barbie products, our people developed a Barbie Fan Club, through which we communicated a good grooming message to children and hoped to win favor with parents. Ultimately, there were allegedly more members in the Barbie Fan Club than there were in the Girl Scouts of America (more than a million). We conceived of a full-color magazine for Barbie buyers, sent them birthday wishes, and provided a Barbie column full of good tips for children to newspapers throughout the country.

Ruth and Elliott Handler, who started Mattel with a $20,000 investment, ultimately were forced out of the company. Ruth and her internal financial advisor, Seymour Rosenberg, were indicted and almost went to jail for allegedly trying to manipulate the price of the company's stock. Shortly after the company had gone public, I tried to convince the Handlers not to display the daily activities of their stock on a bulletin board outside their offices. You'll turn into a stock touting outfit, not a creative toy company, I argued. I wish I hadn't been so prescient.

We also began to become more active in our nation's capital, recognizing the amount of consumer legislation that was being enacted affecting most of our clients. We got Mattel involved in the deliberations of toy safety groups in Washington. In some cases we arranged for our clients to testify before congressional committees. Representing all kind of clients, we had our Washington people develop an early warning system to alert our clients to legislation potentially affecting their businesses. We also picked up Washington-based business and were hired by Amtrak to publicize the new national railroad system.

One day I received a call from California financier Aaron Clark asking whether I would be interested in offering public relations guidance (*pro bono* of course) to the new chairman of the Securities & Exchange Commission in Washington. His name was Harold Williams. I leaped at the chance, knowing it couldn't hurt our business to have that kind of experience and connection. Harold and I worked together for several years, and continued to do so when he left government and became president of the Getty Trust in Los Angeles.

Our firm was not identified as a political public relations firm, although we got involved in an occasional campaign. I acted as an unofficial advisor to Illinois Senator Charles Percy and our people in New York worked for years for Senator Jacob Javits. One day Senator Javits asked us to take on the regional campaign of a young Republican who was mayor of a small Long Island town in New York. We almost got him elected as supervisor of Nassau County against an entrenched Democrat. Governor Rockefeller was so impressed with his (our?) campaign he appointed our client to the Supreme Court bench in New York. His name was Sol Wachtler who, unfortunately, is now a convicted felon as a result of a bizarre extramarital love affair that sent him into disgrace and a jail term. At the time of his fall from grace, he was Chief Justice of the New York Supreme Court and on his way to possibly being governor of the state. CBS was so intrigued with our campaign it did a documentary of our approach on a one-hour special on prime time narrated by Eric Sevareid.

During my alleged retirement years, although no longer involved with my previous firm, I have kept active in public relations matters, taking on interesting assignments that intrigue me.

One such assignment was to develop creative marketing ideas for the Mayfair Hotel in New York. In the course of my research, I realized that no hotel had ever asked me what kind of pillow I preferred. Out of that came the "Pillow Bank" wherein the Mayfair offered guests a brochure illustrating more than a dozen available pillows. Your favorite pillow was to be on your bed the next time you checked in. Offered were down, feather, king-size foam, wing, feather neck, snore stopper, hypoallergenic facial, and other assorted pillows. Looking for a fresh idea in New York hotels, the *New York Times* gave the idea a full-page story in its Sunday magazine.

I am proud that to this day I have had more than a quarter-century-long counseling relationship with Mitchell Energy & Development, Inc., a Big Board company in Houston, Texas. George Mitchell, chairman and president of this large land development and energy company, calls me his PR guru, even though he has a sizable and capable public relations department. George conceived of the idea of a planned new city north of Houston, called The Woodlands, and today more than forty thousand people live in George's beautiful new town. I have also been involved in the development of a citywide hospitality program for Galveston, Texas, where Mitchell Energy has extensive hotel and real estate interests.

The question that has come up most often over the years was how we, a Chicago-based public relations firm, landed the most prestigious account in Hollywood and held it for about thirty years.

It started when I went to see the Academy of Motion Pictures & Sciences about trying to secure an Oscar for our client, Bausch & Lomb Optical Company, for their development of the wide-screen lens used in the picture *The Robe*.

The executive director of the academy, Margaret Herrick, patiently explained that you don't ask for an Oscar; you earn it. She must have been intrigued by my naive approach and

tion, attending special events such as news conferences, speaking in public, and researching and evaluating a variety of materials. PRSA's website contains many well-written and up-to-date articles for those with an interest in the field of PR. A well-known national practitioner summed up the prospects of public relations as follows:

> The future looks good for public relations. It's a growing field primarily because organizations realize that good, strong interrelationships among all groups—employees, shareholders, customers, government, opinion leaders—are essential to their survival and welfare. Also, the increasing sophistication of communications technology demands increasing attention to the integrity of what is communicated, as well as how it is communicated.

Another watershed mark for the advancement and sophistication of public relations occurred following World War II. It was then that experts in the field realized that it was becoming imperative for everybody to have specific, higher education. This necessity became increasingly evident during the subsequent years.

Throughout the 1950s, during and following the Korean War, as American industry began blossoming and the need for an accompanying system of professional public relations became apparent, many independent public relations firms began expanding appreciably. Services for aiding American corporations with their marketing efforts through expert communication and persuasion techniques were becoming greatly in demand.

The trend continued in the United States into the 1960s and beyond. But there was another phenomenon during this period that also enhanced the role of public relations. With the war in Vietnam and the Civil Rights movement, Americans from all walks of life began to emphasize the need for exact and clear communication. Also, given the fervent antiwar sentiment, coupled with wide disbelief in government policy and official statements, it was necessary for people on all sides of the issue to learn a great deal about communicating clearly. Consequently, a wider network of communication specialists, especially in the public relations area, was spawned.

WHAT A PUBLIC RELATIONS FIRM DOES TODAY

While the thrust for press attention is still at the core of most public relations campaigns, publicity being the most powerful public relations tool, the modern-day public relations firm is organized along expanded lines, calling for specialists of all kinds. From a seat-of-the-pants opportunistic function, today's public relations has grown into an organized professional discipline calling for extensive research into objectives, demographics, and potential tools of communications.

Following is a summary of the specialty areas commonly addressed by the modern-day public relations firm:

1. *Corporate Public Relations.* Corporate performance is among the most critical areas in which public relations skills and strategies can make a contribution. A corporation is a financial structure that enables managers to perform needed

functions in society; the stated goals of these managers give character and leadership to the corporation. It is within this dimension of corporate planning that systematic and mature public relations counsel performs a valuable service. Corporate and financial public relations planning starts with the definition of a company's purpose and character. A thoughtful, well-organized program is then created to present the company's profile to investors, analysts, bankers, institutional portfolio managers, editors, civic and government officials, and other key audiences.

We worked for both large and small publicly owned companies. Areas of involvement included counseling on corporate strategic plans, mergers, and acquisitions; identity programs; and other significant events that affect corporate progress.

Staff members included specialists in all corporate relations activities. They wrote and designed annual and quarterly reports, planned annual meetings, arranged presentations to analyst groups, scheduled speaking engagements at business and financial forums, maintained relations with the business media, helped establish liaison between federal and state legislators, and worked with executives in preparing policy statements, position papers, articles, and other published materials.

2. *Marketing Public Relations.* In public relations marketing, the goal is to reach segmented audiences and prompt purchasing decisions.

Aggressive, sales-generating campaigns stimulate brand-name awareness for many of the world's best-known consumer, industrial, and professional products and services—

from airlines, automobiles, beer, and cameras to pharmaceuticals, sunglasses, toys, and X-ray equipment.

Marketing public relations campaigns are designed to complement other promotional activities. Generating test-market attention, extending the impact of advertising themes, and communicating sales messages to segmented audiences are examples of marketing public relations strategies.

As a results-oriented organization, we developed promotional activities to support specific marketing objectives. These included new approaches to retail store and shopping mall promotions, dramatic demonstration projects for consumer and industrial products, promotional tie-ins with celebrities, and media relations programs to achieve extensive news coverage.

3. *Public Affairs and Government Relations.* The majority of our clients conducted their affairs in the public arena. They affirmed this by their decision to retain public relations counsel for assistance in planning and implementing communications programs. Such organizations are especially sensitive to the social, economic, and political forces that shape society.

The public affairs staff in our agency included experts with experience in politics, government operations, and public-issues analysis. The firm's capabilities in these critical areas were enhanced by a well-established Washington, DC, office.

We were experienced in planning and conducting broadly based as well as narrowly targeted communications programs. Activities ranged from grass-roots efforts to campaigns aimed at generating mass support for significant national issues. Topical concerns have included energy issues, consumer affairs, government deregulation, environmental protection, occupational safety, resource recovery, public lands development, and many others. We also specialized in the creation of institutional and advocacy advertising in print and broadcast media to reach target audiences and achieve public affairs objectives. We created campaigns as well as managed all aspects of their implementation.

4. *Broadcast Communications.* In the large agency, the broadcast communications division staff includes professionals with experience as TV and radio news reporters, writers, filmmakers, directors, and broadcast producers.

The production of television and radio features is the division's primary responsibility. Millions of TV viewers across the country regularly watch video news features that are syndicated by PR agencies' own networks of TV stations and cable television systems. The unit also creates documentary films as well as full-length features for corporate and marketing communications uses, including employee relations, sales training, and industrial demonstrations.

The broadcast communications staff also develops and conducts personalized media training workshops for client executives and other spokespersons. The workshops help participants understand electronic media and prepare for news interviews, especially on television, through videotaped role-playing and simulated interviews.

Other assignments include developing concepts for TV and radio programming; scheduling interviews for client spokespersons on national and local broadcast news shows, talk shows, and public affairs programs; and arranging video teleconferences between various locations through satellite television facilities.

5. *Visual Communications.* Color, type, shape, size, illustration, dimension, photography—all of these design considerations require clear thought and analysis before they are joined together to create a distinct form of communication. Once knowledge is gained, only then can ideas be translated into visual imagery that communicates in a stimulating and informative way to achieve a desired purpose.

A full-service graphic arts center creates corporate identity and visual identification systems; collateral materials, including annual reports, brochures, posters, and booklets; logotypes and other symbols for special events; promotional materials, such as point-of-purchase displays and three dimensional exhibits; and broadcast animation for television programming.

Corporate, institutional, and public affairs advertising is another specialty. In addition to the conceptual development of a campaign's graphic theme and the production of advertisements, the company also handles campaign execution.

The daily interaction between the design staff and account managers sharpens sensitivities between both groups and increases understanding about the relationship of design to other communications techniques.

POWER IN MARKETING

In fact, today one can speak of public relations not as a fringe item, but a power in marketing—a source of energy that makes everything else in the marketing machinery work smoother and more efficiently and produces greater results. Marketing management no longer regards public relations as a competitor to advertising and promotion for budget allocations. Rather, public relations is recognized as basic in overall marketing strategy and a useful adjunct to promotion, but it also performs certain functions all its own.

Let's examine some of these unique functions more closely. First, public relations is the market maker. It builds new arenas of demand for advertising and promotion to sell within.

Think about that. What is it that convinces women that they just must have a certain skirt length, a certain neckline, or a certain shoe style next fall or spring? Is it advertising? Is it displays in the store windows? No. These come after something else: the showings in Paris, Rome, and New York duly covered by the fashion version of foreign correspondents and by camerapersons—appropriately displayed on television, in women's magazines, and on fashion pages in the newspapers.

Or take the automobile industry. Did you learn about the new VW Bug first in a television commercial or a display ad? No, you probably learned about it through your newspaper, or possibly in a so-called men's magazine. Perhaps you remember a prerelease article outlining the Bug's features.

Sometimes public relations can expand the market for a product by creating for it a use that never existed before. We did just that for the California Avocado Advisory Board, a marketing group. Tropical fruits of all sorts have received similar promotional pushes.

Some years ago, it was predictable that the prices of avocados, considered somewhat as a connoisseur's food item, would rise. To ensure the maintenance of high demand, despite price levels, we recommended taking advantage of the current interest in natural cosmetics by turning the nutritious avocado into a formula for facials and hair treatments. This, we believed, would also cast the avocado as a heroine of inflation, because the prices of cosmetics and beauty preparations also were climbing. A fifty-nine-cent avocado would be a tremendous bargain for four luxurious beauty treatments—or, as our publicity pointed out, for even one beauty treatment plus a free salad.

Beauty editors from top women's interest and general publication magazines were invited to a luncheon in a "Garden of Eden" that we had created in Manhattan. We covered a model with avocado cosmetic preparations and developed dozens of other story angles. A well-known skin expert spoke on the health benefits of this natural cosmetic. We selected Gunilla Knutson, author of two books on natural beauty, as a spokeswoman and arranged for her to demonstrate what was called the "Green Grocer Facial" on a syndicated national television show—for fifty minutes!

We prepared illustrated features on the avocado facial for women's pages of newspapers and homemaker shows on television. We made a radio transcription, using Beverly Garland. And, we developed a set of syndicated beauty recipes for suburban newspapers. Among the notable results were take-out features, which appeared in the same month in *Vogue* and *Harper's Bazaar. Seventeen* also carried a feature, as did *Woman's Homelife.* Our syndicated television show appeared on thirty-seven stations. What were the results of all this? It built a rising crescendo of avocado demand over the six months before the related advertising appeared.

MARKETING CREDIBILITY

Public relations establishes marketing credibility. It validates the claims being made for a product or service. When a sales effort is made—on the TV, on the radio, on the Internet, or in person—you can't help being something of a skeptic, can you? Of course, the pitch is going to tell you that this particular product works best and everyone is a satisfied customer. If salespeople didn't talk like that, they would have no chance of earning any commissions.

But when you read about that same product—or see it endorsed by one of your favorite television personalities or syndicated columnists—your skepticism is diluted.

When you come across an advertisement that interests you, you may well believe its claims enough to respond to it. But you will respond a lot quicker if you have just heard by word-of-mouth or in the newspapers how convenient or how reasonable or how delicious this product has proved to be for someone else.

Even if the publicity isn't signed, there is an implied endorsement by the editor who, you feel sure, would not allow anything unverified or incomplete to occupy editorial space or time in his or her media. To earn this confidence, publicity must be handled with a professional sense of journalistic integrity, with a concentration on facts and on newsmaking qualities that meet the requirements of the editor. Recognition of this has made product and service publicity almost as accepted a source of editorial material for publications as a wire service or a crew of reporters.

I once went through the Atlanta *Journal* to check for examples of marketing public relations and found quite a few. The marketing of oysters profited from a full-page picture feature on oyster fishing. There was a three-column picture marketing some new unisex trousers called baggies. Wine marketing was the real purpose for running a feature story on an auction. There was a two-page feature marketing pork—how to buy and serve it. And all these other marketing subjects drew one or more citations: automobiles, parsnips, airlines, frozen foods, cookies, pickles, potatoes, pancakes, poultry, cheese, chocolate, cabbage, almonds, yogurt, bread, computers, and a television set special.

Public relations supplies welcome mats for the salesperson. One is more willing to open the door when the salesperson who is knocking is bringing a product or service that is somewhat familiar and, suddenly, more interesting.

If a man has read an advisory column of the financial page about how insurance best fits into a retirement program and has turned to his wife and said, "This is the kind of policy we ought to have," they may be willing to send in that direct mail postcard for a free pocket diary that they know will bring an insurance salesperson along with it.

Public relations also generates increased impact at the point of purchase. When a retailer knows that a product he or she sells is going to be seen by hundreds of prospective customers on a local television show or read about in the newspapers, he or she is much more disposed to increase inventory, take advantage of cooperative advertising offers, and arrange more shelf space and better store displays.

Reprints of colorful newspaper and magazine features that remind shoppers of an interesting idea they have seen—or attract their attention if they haven't seen it before—make particularly good window posters and counter cards. Reprints also are useful as billing stuffers and direct mail pieces.

Many trade and some consumer magazines contain reply cards with which further information on items publicized in them may be requested. These cards can be keyed for return to salespersons and distributors.

CRISIS COMMUNICATIONS

Perhaps nothing proves the need for professional public relations more than the handling of corporations and institutions in moments of crisis. When the Hyatt Hotel suffered a disaster in Kansas City, the parent organization's public relations people were on a plane immediately after the disaster, drafting press releases and statements while still in flight. They hit the ground running.

The Tylenol case, when three people were poisoned by violated capsules, was a remarkable public relations reversal of what could have been a permanent disaster affecting a successful brand name. Public relations professionals were in the thick of that campaign. Johnson and Johnson, makers of Tylenol, recalled thirty million bottles of extra-strength Tylenol, even though the corporation believed the poisoned capsules were in a limited marketing area.

Under the heading of crisis communications might be listed the experience of Memphis, Tennessee, following the assassination there of Dr. Martin Luther King. The community leaders realized that because of the assassination, Memphis had suffered a severe blow to its image and hired our firm to set in motion programs of positive public relations. Our client was the Association of Commerce, and we opened an office there to work on the account. We were also called in to help with the press coverage of the trial of convicted killer Earle Ray Jones.

We also got involved somewhat marginally in the wake of the assassination of President John F. Kennedy. The rifle used by Lee Harvey Oswald was purchased from the direct mail division of Klein's Chicago sporting goods chain. With the FBI exploring his records and the press swarming over this store, owner Milton Klein asked us to take over press relations. Klein was asked by the FBI not to talk to the press until the record of the gun purchase could be confirmed.

Today many corporations have developed disaster programs in anticipation of emergencies. Under those circumstances, it's important to centralize press response and to be sure that the executives involved know how to respond to press inquiries. We preached open and candid response.

A SAMPLE PUBLICITY TIMETABLE

Marketing publicity is flexible and can be molded to a strategic timetable, city by city. For example, a plan for a twice-a-year major toy company publicity blitz to be personally conducted in twenty key toy markets might work as follows:

Select a personable toy consultant from the toy company staff and work with that person to develop interview story lines that fit the parental concerns: how to look for safety in toys or how to use them for furthering education in the home.

Book interviews in advance by telephone and by mail stating that this toy expert will be in town for two or three days and is prepared to discuss and demonstrate toy topics and new toy developments. This technique capitalizes on the growing trend of local media to reach for national personalities in local settings in order to compete more successfully with the national media.

Upon arriving in a major city, the expert's itinerary is booked with interviews on television and radio talk shows, homemaker shows, and listener call-in programs, as well as with the women's editors of newspapers and local columnists. Suggest in advance the types of questions that will generate interesting responses or add something to interpretations of current news, like what's happening in the consumer movement. Distribute a press kit including such items as a background corporate report on the toy company, a fact sheet, a description of new toy refinements, color transparencies for Sunday newspaper editions, and other items to stimulate ideas.

Planned interview topics lead naturally to the use of toys and to illustrate points. Show, for example, how the company goes to the extra expense to sew a bow on a doll instead of using a pin. Test marketing also can be adapted to this key market procedure.

Thus the general procedures of the profession may be used in marketing a particular product or service. One thing should be clear: Selling a product involves a great deal of preparation, both in advance and at the point of purchase.

CHAPTER 7

MANY MARKETS, MANY ROLES

The functions of a public relations person are infinite. The specialist may be asked to promote an idea or sell almost any type of product. He or she must be ready, often on a moment's notice, to come up with a saleable plan that will get results for the firm.

Betsy Plank, formerly Illinois Bell Telephone's assistant vice president for public relations, has been in the field more than thirty years and has offered a clear summary of the different roles played by the public relations expert. According to Ms. Plank:

> The field has a wide range of practice. It includes counsel to management, community relations, research and identification of issues, employee communications, consumer relations, public affairs, investor and financial relations, and marketing public relations.

The skills of public relations specialists can be utilized by nearly every segment of society. Holders of public office, for example, as well as local, ad hoc community organizations, emphasize up-to-date techniques in communication and persuasion. And improving community relations is of primary importance to all of them. Businesses, small and large, avail themselves of most of the skills of public relations specialists to show potential consumers that they will benefit from purchasing and using the product.

A product must be good, or in the long run large numbers of people will not repeatedly purchase it. But no matter how good the product, if it is not sold properly—if the message regarding its high quality is not carefully presented—even the best product will not approach its potential sales volume. Ultimate profit is a two-way street on which these two equally important factors must travel side by side.

Communicating to the consumer, to create and continue a favorable impression, is crucial for all types of products. This includes breakfast cereals and cola, which have frequent resales, and expensive, infrequently replaced products like automobiles.

Communication and advocacy are crucial and interrelated functions of the public relations specialist. He or she must not only communicate a message to the potential consumer in a clear, concise, and gripping fashion but also convince the consumer to purchase or use the product or service that the client is selling. The message is not intended to be neutral. It is advocating a specific point of view: what the client is trying to sell is better or preferable to those of competing companies that are also trying to sell their products or services to the same publics.

Being successful is not easy. There is a great deal of competition. Makers and sellers of competing products, too, utilize the skills of public relations practitioners.

Prior to putting out a marketing campaign for a particular product, a public relations person must do a great deal of study, research, and hard thinking. As we've stated before, today's world is very, very complicated, and it gets more complex daily.

Consequently, ascertaining how to reach the separate publics is more difficult than it was a few decades or so ago, when modern society was not so diverse and complicated. The public relations specialist must first identify and accurately define the public or publics that he or she intends to reach and then select the tools and techniques with which to reach them.

Keep in mind that no matter what product one wishes to sell, there is an abundance of good competition out there trying just as hard to attract the consumer's dollar. Therefore, in order to make an appreciable impact, one must pinpoint exactly where and how to act. In ascertaining how to be effective, one must wear many hats. Having sophisticated knowledge and expertise in public relations is essential, but that alone does not suffice. What about psychology, sociology, and motivational research? In fact, thorough knowledge of all the social and behavioral sciences is advisable, and at times, even essential.

MANY DIFFERENT PUBLICS

One must know the demographics now and have an accurate idea of what they will be in the future. Today, the United States is becoming a nation of the young and the old. Much of what is being marketed is directed heavily to these two groups, at opposite ends of the chronological scale. Depending on the product, of course, certain characteristics should and should not be highlighted.

Certain products have obvious appeal to some groups and no appeal to others. For example, no public relations expert would direct a motor bike marketing effort to the elderly; on the other hand, it would be a mistake to exclude from the sales campaign and promotion the large segment of middle-aged Americans, because such a bike is not only appealing to the teenager who is out to have fun. Many baby boomers pride themselves on their youthfulness and are eager to spend time outdoors. Many bike owners are near retirement and plan to ride more as they have more time.

Consequently, a public relations specialist for a motor bike company would probably choose not to restrict a campaign to rock stars extolling the virtues of riding bikes along the Pacific Coast highway. The campaign also must be directed to the young at heart.

AGE GROUPING

Devising a single promotional campaign won't work. There must be at least two: one to reach the young Generation Xers, and another for the older, professionally successful "baby boomer" set. Once it has been decided that more than one effort is in order, the professional public relations person must determine, within certain age limits, toward which aspects of the consumers to direct his or her efforts—education, economic status, snob appeal, desire for upward mobility, or other areas.

The number of factors that must be considered and analyzed are virtually unlimited. For each separate group within a certain age or economic category, one approach may appeal while another will not. However, it is impossible to set up a widespread campaign that incorporates every favorable aspect for each separate entity within a general category. Therefore, the specialist must pick and choose—disposing of some thrusts and making use of others.

OLDER AMERICANS

Already, even with the unheard-of success of youth-oriented movies and video games, there are signs that previously youth-oriented industries are not doing as well as they used to. American society is getting older and older; there are fewer and fewer young people.

We have already seen a great increase in products directed to the older American. Denture cleaners are advertised often on television. Aspirin, when advertised on television or in newspapers, doesn't concentrate only on relieving headaches. Relief for arthritis is at least as heavily emphasized. Makeup creams to hide wrinkles rival soft-drink ads in terms of frequency. One sporting goods company is marketing a golf club directed solely to the older American. They predict that it will "allow the mature golfer to get the ball up in the air faster."

In trying to determine the internal and external motivations of consumers in the early years of this century, public relations specialists must bear in mind that the United States is becoming an increasingly older society. Consequently, attitudes of these older Americans will help determine what marketing strategies should be used.

According to the U.S. Census Bureau, people 85 years of age and older are now a rapidly growing age group, with their population increasing by over 34 percent between 1990 and 1998, to total about 1 million elderly folks. The baby boomers are aging, with the 45–64 age group showing a 24 percent increase, which equates to about 11.1 million people. Compare that growth to the small increase in children from birth to 17; they grew only 9.3 percent, to equal about 5.9 million children. Meanwhile the 18–44 age group showed only a 1.1 percent increase, which equates to roughly 1.2 million people. These are the kind of statistics to which public relations professionals will have to pay attention in the coming years.

As a result of this graying of America, all professionals will have to understand what older people want and how to help them realize it. Naturally, in medicine, gerontology (the study of aging) will be required of medical students and physicians, but other people, like public relations experts, also will have to know a great deal about elderly Americans.

ETHNIC GROUPINGS

Not only are appeals not universal in terms of age groups, but they are different in respect to regions of the country—city versus rural and even neighborhood to neighborhood within an urban area.

Advertising also takes these differences into account. Billboards directed primarily at black Americans, for example, often feature black actors and actresses as role models. Advertisements for the same product would not be used in most rural areas. Ethnicity, too, often plays a role in deciding where and how to direct marketing efforts. For example, it was very common to see displays for a particular brand of Jewish rye bread at subway stops through New York City, but a few miles out of the metropolitan area the displays were no longer in evidence.

Throughout the nation, there have been significant increases in the Hispanic population. Projections for the coming years show that this trend will continue.

According to the U.S. Census Bureau, the nation's Hispanic population increased from 22.4 million in 1990 to 30.3 million in 1998, a gain of 35.2 percent or almost 8 million people. California, Texas, Florida, New York, and Arizona all saw large increases in their Hispanic populations. It is important to note that Hispanics may be of any race. Thirty million people constitute a segment of the overall U.S. population that must be taken seriously.

The total Hispanic population of Los Angeles is second to New York's, and two-thirds of Miami's residents are Hispanic. One-fifth of Chicago is Hispanic. Reciting these statistics is not done primarily to offer a census-type ranking. The numbers make a significant point: Hispanic Americans no longer live only in the Southwest and California. And marketing experts, which we as public relations professionals are, must keep that in mind.

Producers of products have begun concentrating efforts in these regions on the impact of these groups as consumers. The so-called "browning of America" has already begun. Efforts to reach these new consumers have also started and will be positively expanded throughout the decade.

As is the case with other races and ethnic groups, Hispanics cannot be categorized simply. They do not fit neatly into one socioeconomic group. Some, unfortunately, are not well educated and work at relatively menial jobs. Others have partaken of the American dream and must be appealed to in the same fashion as other middle- and upper-class, economically successful, and educated Americans.

To remain ignorant of these and other key demographic changes would be tantamount to missing the essence of public relations, as it performs an invaluable role to marketing in America in the future.

CHAPTER 8

PUBLIC RELATIONS TODAY AND TOMORROW

Although marketing comprises the lion's share of the public relations specialist's activities, it by no means represents the sole area in which he or she works. We have emphasized that the inseparable companions of marketing for anyone in public relations are persuasion and communication. Without these skillfully used components, there would be no public relations as it exists at its highest level of skill and sophistication.

We also have stressed the fact that it is a necessity to help clients make a reasonable profit in their businesses. As public relations experts, we serve corporate America in performing a much needed and worthwhile purpose. We and corporate clients need each other, and neither of us should lose sight of that fact.

Although we have already discussed the primary roles that marketing plays, there are additional contributions that must not go unnoticed. For example, public relations is the hook with which specific marketing goals can be attached to news interests. When a beautiful, well-appointed cruise ship sails out of or into port, it is news—but only if you make it news.

Making news applies to a wide range of subjects. More than a decade ago, our firm introduced a special project of broad consumer interest, "The Auditory Environment in the Home." Under a grant from one of our clients, the leading manufacturer of stereo headphones, we approached a graduate department at the University of Wisconsin that had produced a completely objective study that warned that noise levels in the home were high, were going higher, were potentially dangerous, and were being ignored.

These findings were announced at a creative news conference in New York, and a psychiatrist was retained to interpret the findings in terms of individual emotional and mental stress. Our client's president outlined reasons for his firm's involvement and called for action from fellow manufacturers, architects, and interior designers. Brochures reprinting the speeches of the news meeting were distributed to influential people in industry; federal, state, and local government; trade and professional associations; ecology-minded organizations; and the financial community.

The response was tremendous. The *New York Times* and many national magazines ran stories. There were 150 requests for copies of the entire study and nearly 2,000 women's clubs from around the United States wrote for a program.

Public relations can often reach into the marketing areas where direct sales won't penetrate. For example, a salesperson may not be able to arrange an appointment with a physician to tell him or her about a new drug. On the other hand, through medical journals, public relations can obtain direct, easy access to the physician. Thus the physician learns about the new drug without contact with the salesperson.

With a booming economy marked by high rates of employment, many industries have been working hard to hire and keep employees. The costs of advertising and general merchandising have been increasing, so the product managers must have help to get nationwide coverage.

In this situation, marketing publicity is important. Furthermore, in enlarging the public impact of the product message, it can and does improve the productivity of the advertising dollar. PR is no longer seen as a tactic; successful companies now know that it is a key strategy for growth and long-term survival.

We do not have to be reminded that we live in an age of discontent and dissent and disbelief, which throws suspicion on the advertising, packaging, and sales claims made for products. There may be no way to reassure the consumer other than by demonstrating the product or by letting the consumer read about the product's benefits in an editorial setting.

Public relations also gives valuable feedback from the arbiters of social taste and consumer spending habits. When you plan a marketing public relations program, you are, in a very real sense, conducting a market research project. You contact those editors and commentators who report regularly to the buyers of your product. These are the people who must be attracted to your product, not only because they buy it themselves, but also because they have status as thought leaders.

Product producers will be trying out their ideas on such communicators and getting valuable feedback. Furthermore, they can ask questions about the market and can be certain of receiving objective opinions. These people can appraise your markets with more accuracy than any other source—even better than the consumers themselves.

Marketing is a powerful tool, which must be properly utilized for maximum effectiveness. As public relations specialists, we must admonish corporate leaders to make public relations product publicity a part of their total marketing plan; they must realize that these are essential components. Public relations must be given a place at the conference table, from the very beginning. The public relations and advertising persons must be teammates, not rivals, who are dedicated to the same mission.

We are convincing the highest echelon of corporate America not to cheat public relations in the marketing budget. It may buy more for the buck, but it buys nothing unless it is done by experienced, bright, and creative people—and that means well-paid people. Employers are demanding more knowledge of their industry from prospective, public relations practitioners, but they usually are willing to pay for the right package of skills and knowledge.

Public relations has come to be just as attractively designed and packaged as anything else in the sales kit. The entire job must be done with the highest level of expertise, because that is always the most effective, and, therefore, economical way to do it.

Public relations and marketing, too, must be sold or merchandised, and that is at least as important as merchandising a final product. Without selling good public relations and top-flight marketing, a firm cannot adequately sell its product. Don't take anything for granted. Keep selling yourself and the products. Get the word out that you are good at public relations.

Use public relations as the primary vehicle for marketing both yourself and products. It is the power that makes the difference.

FINDING YOUR NICHE

For the bright, articulate person, public relations is an extremely inviting field offering a wide variety of employment opportunities.

Although we have accentuated the role of the public relations specialist as it relates to the corporate world, we have also made it clear that there are many other avenues along which the public relations person may travel. These include public affairs, community relations, public information, media relations, public opinion surveying, government relations, financial or investor relations, political campaigns, consumer affairs, and the ever-growing area of research and statistics.

In all these areas, the old adage concerning public relations holds true. "PR" means Performance and Recognition. Especially in the intangible areas of communications and persuasion it is necessary for those entering public relations to be able to decide upon a precise desired result and to develop strategies to obtain it. One must be able to ascertain whether he or she has achieved the desired result. After all, if the professional public relations person is unable to interpret what he or she did, then why and how can a client support the program?

We need more professionals in the field of public relations who know and can explain why they're doing what they're doing, and they must have the knowledge and skills to interpret the "what" and "why" for their clients.

We need more professionals who know how to assess the winds of change and who can serve as a two-way conduit of understanding between the client and the public. There are still too many public relations people who act like the old-time stunt pilots—flying by the seat of their pants without a compass or a flight plan.

CLIENT-SPECIALIST RELATIONS

Public relations specialists encounter some obstacles even when they approach an assignment with excellent planning and foresight. For example, in many cases, your client is a nonbeliever. He or she is unsure about how much good your services can do. As always, you have to sell yourself as well as your services.

Unless you do your planning early, you will begin with uncoordinated perceptions. It is to your advantage, and the client's, to plan ahead. A public relations effort must be launched with mutually agreed-upon objectives: agree on what publics your client wants to reach, the tools of communication to be used, and the yardsticks for measuring the results.

Client and public relations advisor both must be measuring the same thing. They must agree before, during, and after a communications program on targets and objectives.

A good public relations program must insist on setting up a reporting system that is consistent and on a face-to-face basis. Face-to-face meetings go a long way in the constant educational process. Written reports emphasize the "what"; face-to-face meetings add the dimension of the "why." More nuances of understanding are possible in an instant feedback situation.

Coupled with this, of course, is the need for the communicator to know exactly what he or she is doing and to know how to market his or her results. Without this, a perfunctory reading of your public relations reports is going to get even more perfunctory. No matter one's lack of understanding about public relations, the efficient executive, above all, has a respect for clarity of communication. In our firm, we used detailed flowcharts that were reviewed and updated constantly; the charts showed objectives, publics to be reached, and the tools of communication that were to be utilized.

Analyze your results in terms of the desired goal or reach of the specific campaign. Check your television, radio, Internet, and print efforts early and often to make sure that they are on target with what you and your client set out to achieve.

The most important use of clippings and other tangible results—other than to indicate to the client that the public relations person is functioning properly—is to stimulate the organization to great efforts. Such results have an emotional impact; they provide a successful consciousness that spurs people to greater efforts.

How do you measure results? You can hire a good research organization to do before-and-after studies, which ties in well with the involvement of management in setting objectives. You also can construct your own evaluation of your image and run surveys before, during, and after specific efforts. And, of course, don't forget the press. Ask key editors covering your specific field what they see as your organization's key image and what they see as problem areas. See if their assessment agrees with yours. If it doesn't, you may have to come up with a new objective.

Ask yourself what you're doing correctly? What is going wrong? What more should you do? Sometimes, along with good, objective advice, you get personal bias. Take that into account. The end result will be a greater capacity to see yourself as others see you—a necessary gift for all public relations practitioners.

For newcomers into the field, this discussion about measuring performance may sound a bit like putting the cart before the horse. However, I believe that by sharing some of my observations you may avoid pitfalls and become better practitioners of your newly found art than you otherwise would have been.

PUBLIC RELATIONS AND NEW TECHNOLOGY

Electronics to Revolutionize PR Business[1]
by Richard E. Rotman

Public relations as a marketing discipline has been surprisingly resistant to technological progress, yet it has flourished despite its low tech orientation. But emerging are changes that may force public relations practitioners to alter their businesses, or lose ground to a new group of service providers who have grasped the new technology.

Traditionally a field with low capital expenditures, public relations has thrived because strong personal relations with those in the media have often meant more to success than a scientific approach. Practitioners can easily work out of homes, with just a telephone, computer, and fax. Advertising expenditures, too, have always dwarfed those of public relations, and the largest advertising agencies are far larger than the biggest PR firms, most of which are in fact owned by worldwide agency networks.

Two developments, however, loom large with potential for revolutionizing the public relations business. The first, of course, is the information highway, and the second is CD-based technology. That hoary old PR staple, the news release, sent out by fax, courier, and newswire, could easily be a thing of the distant low tech past.

---

[1]Reprinted with the permission of *Marketing* magazine, Toronto, Canada.

Many in North America now enjoy:

- A modem in every newsroom; news release distribution from computer-to-computer; PR practitioner to reporter, without the intervention of hard copy. Very few PR firms operate without such essential features as fax modems and on-line services at each desk. Some high-tech PR pros use media lists based on Internet- or CompuServe-type addresses, not necessarily compiled by the practitioners but by the reporter's placing himself or herself on an interest list to receive such material. The potential for E-mail interview questions at all hours of the day is also appealing, especially since voice mail's use by busy journalists often blocks the all-important personal touch.

- Interactive CD-based news releases, which not only tell the product story but also provide video, interviews, different perspectives, and downloadable copy and art. Other CD-based potentials include virtually unlimited background capabilities, so that diligent researchers can delve more deeply into background information, based on keyword searching. Creating one of these is still somewhat expensive, at least for now, but will no doubt become more common as technology improves.

- Forums, databases, and live on-line product discussions are a new target audience, and despite Internet users' biases against commercialization, the day is already at hand in which company CEOs and product spokespersons can place themselves in an on-line forum, answering questions and engaging in dialogue not only with media but directly with end users. Developments like these clearly reduce the media's historic role as mediator between companies and consumers.

• Direct-to-home communications that bypass media directly are an expansion of the forum opportunities. But instead of traditional publications that filter, edit, and revise news releases, consumers may elect to receive material on a subject of interest directly, through on-line addresses, reducing the need for media covering new cars, electronics, health, or a number of other topics.

• Worldwide television lifts product announcements and news conferences across continents. Very few PR firms can produce a television news release as easily as a printed one. However, satellite downlinks, which only television stations can now afford, will become commonplace in the future, opening the potential to reach homes directly, all around the world. Why wouldn't a computer enthusiast, for example, wish to experience a product announcement news conference as it was happening instead of reading about it in the press? Why will a reporter need to attend a future press conference when it is available on his or her own combined computer/TV screen? (Verifying electronic attendance to clients speaking into television cameras in an empty room will be an interesting test of PR firms' credibility.)

For PR firms and corporate departments to stay ahead of this microchip-based curve, the best advice is to start in one corner of the office, much like redecorating a room. Pick one computer to enhance, install one modem. Designate one staff member to stay abreast of developments in CDs and interactivity. Then, as new efficiencies result, re-engineer another section, then another person.

Although more established firms may have some financial advantages in this crucial need for restructuring, most are far behind when creating a high-tech future. The firms of tomorrow are those wrestling with the technology today, and they may not resemble anything that is already known in the marketplace. Right now, in basements and garages, small businesses are being created that will provide access to the new technologies, first to agencies and then directly to clients. Those firms will leap to the top of PR trade magazine rankings in the future.

EXPANDED SERVICES AND GROWTH IN PR FIRMS

A Strategic Plan for Growth
by Jesse L. Rotman[*]

For small public relations firms and single-person consultancies, traditional public relations assignments from existing small-business clients often can be a stepping-stone to

---

[*]Jesse L. Rotman is the head of his own public relations and marketing company, The Rooster Group.

broader responsibilities in external and internal communications as well as in marketing activities and even advertising.

The corporate clients these PR firms and professionals serve usually fit the profile of small- to medium-sized companies, often under $200 million in sales, that have little or no internal public relations and marketing capabilities. As the result, they often miss many communications and promotional opportunities or handle them ineffectively.

These companies usually rely on a patchwork of outside agencies and vendors for project-oriented assignments to implement basic marketing and corporate communications services. The company is not achieving "more bang for the buck" as this scattershot approach not only adds to the ultimate cost but also is an inefficient use of resources with all of its added requirements for coordination and indoctrination.

It's also fair to say that few part-time resources will ever understand the client company or organization, its products and services, and its top management as well as the PR counselor who's already in place and providing ongoing services.

NEW BUSINESS DEVELOPMENT STRATEGY

The potential to expand a PR firm's or consultant's role beyond its basic corporate and/or marketing public relations charter is one that every practitioner ought to pursue as a priority new-business development strategy.

Consider that virtually all corporate and marketing communications activities stem from the same wellspring: outstanding copywriting coupled with a "nose for news" to divine what's most marketable about a company. That's clearly the PR professional's forte as well as the likely foundation for the existing client relationship. Thus it is not much of a stretch to apply that underlying expertise and client knowledge to other services under the communications/ marketing umbrella.

THE COMMUNICATIONS AUDIT

Don't let an unfamiliarity with graphics and design or with advertising production and media buying inhibit this potential to grow an existing client relationship into new areas. If necessary, form a strategic alliance with a small graphic-design firm or ad agency to cooperatively reinforce the ability to offer an expanded menu of services.

Conducting a "communications audit" as a special assignment is highly recommended to support the effort to build an expanded relationship. The objective of the audit is to identify a client's corporate and marketing communications opportunities and needs. This process not only serves the PR counselor's business-development objectives, but it also becomes a strategic consulting platform on which to advise a client.

The audit should seek to detail and establish a timeline for a company's full calendar of corporate, financial, sales, marketing, and promotional milestones. The resulting report itemizes timing and functional responsibility for everything from annual shareholder meetings and quarterly financial reports to trade show activities, customer/dealer relations programs, sales meetings, new product introductions, packaging and collateral materials development, and other activities. The ensuing discussion can lead to the realization that there's an economic as well as a productivity benefit from consolidating many of these not-so-disparate corporate and marketing communications activities with one resource.

For the small PR firm or the experienced counselor who operates as a single-person consultancy, this process mirrors the transformation that is taking place among large PR and advertising agencies alike. The lines of specialization are blurring as these firms recast themselves as corporate and marketing communications generalists able to handle everything from the most basic PR/media relations activities to the whole array of advertising and marketing communications activities.

On a smaller scale, this diversification should be a key opportunity for growth for the smaller PR organization. Expanding existing client relationships should always be among any PR firm's highest business development priorities, and the communications audit process presents a strong case for this growth.

THE NEED FOR A LIBERAL ARTS EDUCATION

The demands of public relations are becoming ever more complicated. The competition just to enter the field is getting more intense. One cannot even consider an entry-level job in public relations without a college degree.

Although our computerized world promises to become more complex and mechanically sophisticated in the years to come, very precise technical background is not the only thing aspiring public relations people need. Quite the contrary. We use great time-saving and problem-solving machines, yet we realize more dramatically than ever that no machine can replace the human being with his or her endless capacity to think, solve problems, and communicate in a concise, clear, and intelligent fashion.

Public relations specialists must be able to adapt and react to ever-fluid situations. And there is no better training than a good, solidly based liberal arts education.

In order to succeed, all top-notch public relations specialists must have:

- A keen intellect. The ability to grasp a problem and solve it quickly and follow up with productive actions. One must be able to decide when to and when not to. When a client is wrong, the professional public relations person must have the courage to say so. In the long run, a "yes man" not only does himself or herself a disservice but also allows the client to follow a harmful course of action.
- Empathy. To understand what goal the client wishes to achieve. One has to be able to read between the lines, since oftentimes a client is unwilling, or unable, to articulate exactly what he or she wants to achieve. Once you get a feel for what the client wants, you must also realize why he or she wants it. Again, the need to be part psychologist is recognized.
- Creativity. The entire public relations package, which the specialist makes up and presents to the client, by definition, is creative. If it were not, why would a corpo-

ration or any other customer spend time and money to retain a public relations expert?

• Diplomacy. When talking about public relations, which means dealing with intangibles like creativity and sensitivity, egos often get involved. In fact, they sometimes get in the way of what's to be accomplished. So one has to be careful not to step on the needs for acceptance and self-gratification of the individuals involved. Sometimes balancing the individual needs against those of the entire mission is not easy, but the good public relations specialist must be able to do so.

• Perspective. At all times, the public relations expert must keep in mind that he or she has two primary masters. One is the client who must be satisfied with the work that is being done. At the same time, the public relations person must realize that the final arbiter of social change in our society is the court of public opinion. The public can be very fickle and very fast, and one must be able to switch gears and adapt to quickly changing situations in order to succeed in today's world of public relations.

We do not wish to imply that success in public relations requires a liberal arts education. History, literature, and economics majors, for example, all provide excellent backgrounds. A solid foundation in business administration, as well as in attitude and opinion research, is tremendously helpful to anyone who enters the growing and complex field of public relations. But these specific skills, without the general ability to react properly and quickly, would not serve us well.

It used to be that public relations employers only looked for good writers and communicators and were very willing to teach new hires about the field or business they were entering. Now many employers are looking for people with a background in the "hot" growth areas like health care, and technologies like computers and biotechnology. They are asking for workers who can keep up a hectic pace of work in a complicated market, right from day one. Because there are not as many qualified people as there are positions in many parts of the country, wages and benefit packages have been improving.

That being said, it is important to note that while some highly qualified people are being offered very exciting packages including things like sign-on bonuses and stock options, a shorter corporate "life span" may be part of the deal. Some PR professionals are even finding severance clauses right in the offer letter. As corporations restructure and merge, many public relations departments have been eliminated overnight leaving professionals to reapply for what had recently been "their" positions.

Entry-level salaries in large cities start at about $20,000, with a median income from salary at $45,000. Seasoned professionals may make $75,000 to $150,000 and often have a title of vice president.

For any bright man or woman with skills in communication and persuasion and who writes and speaks English correctly, there is no better field than public relations. It is growing and you can grow with it. A summer of exciting work can become an endless career for all seasons.

SALARIES

In 1997 the median annual income in the industries employing the largest numbers of public relations specialists were:

Management and public relations $35,100
State government, except education
    and hospitals $32,100
Colleges and universities $30,600

According to a salary survey conducted for the Public Relations Society of America, the overall median salary in public relations was about $49,100. Salaries in public relations ranged from less than $22,800 to more than $141,400. There was very little difference among the median salaries for account executives in public relations firms, corporations, government, health care, or nonprofit organizations—all ranged from over $32,000 to nearly $34,000.

Public relations specialists in the federal government in nonsupervisory, supervisory, and managerial positions averaged about $56,700 a year in 1999.

A BUSY DAY IN THE PUBLIC RELATIONS PROFESSION

One way to decide whether a career in public relations is right for you is to read about how someone in the profession spends his or her day. Because my day was only typical of very few individuals—those who are large agency presidents—I asked a senior vice president in our firm to keep a diary of everything he did on one Monday:

7:00 A.M. Read *Chicago Sun-Times,* especially business column. Read *Chicago Tribune,* especially business section and George Lazarus marketing column, containing news of public relations and advertising profession.

8:00 Arrive at work, read *Wall Street Journal* and *New York Times,* must-reads for public relations professionals. Helps you keep up with the national business community of which you are a part.

8:15 Write notes to account executive questioning if project on program for promoting awareness of Alzheimer's disease (early senility) will be completed on time. Also passed on memos concerning First Alert by Pittway, the world's leading manufacturer of smoke detectors, discovered item on Koss Corporation's new video cleaning products in *Video Review* and passed it on to account executive working on that account.

8:30 Drafted budget for project to occur in the next calendar year for Whirlpool Corporation, involving a national opinion study that will be used as a publicity tool and corporate recognition device.

9:25 Asked question concerning availability of staff member and reviewed office charts describing who works on what account and what time might be available to help another executive. Account staff members book an average of 140 hours per month on accounts; some time is occasionally left over.

9:30 Operations Committee. We discuss administrative, sales, and account matters in a frank, open forum. The office is divided into divisions headed by senior or executive vice presidents, and it is these individuals, each of whom have fifteen to twenty-five years experience in the business, who form the group.

We discussed: assignment from New York office. Would involve nearly a third of a person's time for up to one month.

Assignment from same account involving accompanying the company's spokesperson in media interviews in Chicago.

New York assignment from Kinney Shoes to publicize Kinney's cross-country race semifinals for high school students to take place in Hinsdale, Illinois, over Thanksgiving. This race is part of the only truly national cross-country championships for students.

In each case, an individual was selected to work on these public relations campaigns. In some cases, account responsibilities were shifted and time reduced or the remainder was given to someone else.

Looking ahead, we reviewed who might have time available in the upcoming months when present projects were completed. I was assigned to review this for the group.

The weekly office staff meetings were discussed. It was agreed that the meetings ought to be made shorter but continued on a weekly basis. The staff meetings are the one instance when the entire office gathers together and shares experiences, problems, successes, new business, news of clients visiting the office. One decision of the Operations Committee was to make sure the staff meetings recognize the role of the secretary to a greater degree.

10:30 After the meeting, staffing the short-term assignment was again discussed; the senior vice president in charge agreed to accompany the spokesperson himself, as a way to learn more about the product.

11:15 Just as I was about to leave the office to meet a client at the Premium-Incentive Show, he called. Press kits I thought were approved needed changes. We stayed on the telephone for quite some time, revising several stories outlining First Alert by Pittway's role in the premium market. Companies buy premiums to offer as sales incentives—for example, if a salesperson reaches a goal, he or she may be able to pick from a list of rewards, such as First Alert smoke detectors and Apple Computers. Luckily, the client reached me; he did not plan to go to the show, and I would have arrived at the McCormick Place exhibition hall with press kits that could not be used. Although we get to know a company well, the client has the last word on copy because of his or her own deeper involvement with the day-to-day workings of his or her own organization.

11:30 We agreed on changes and they were sent to be made.

11:45 Each year, I teach a public relations course to students at the Francis Parker Evening School. My class last year was particularly successful, and the students have kept up with me, through lunches like today's, by telling me about their career progress.

1:00 Return to the office. The new press kits are ready. I reviewed them and noticed that in being forced to change them so rapidly, the client's first name was left out of one story. We changed the story and restuffed the press kits with the corrected release, and I was off to the show.

1:15 At McCormick Place, I showed the press kit to the company's vice president of sales and marketing, who had asked his colleague to make the changes with me. He appreciated our quick turnaround. First Alert's management supervisor from its advertising agency was also at the show, and we discussed writing a trade press release on advertising plans for the product. A trade press release is circulated to magazines covering a particular industry, i.e., *Retailing Home Furnishings, Mart, Merchandising*. When a retailer reads that a company is launching a major advertising campaign to help him or her sell a product, he or she feels that the company is backing his or her efforts.

Also at the show, I visited three other clients' exhibits. Travel is an important part of the premium and incentive industry, and I visited the Jamaica Tourist Board exhibit. Our client there gave me a very fine Jamaican cigar, rolled before my eyes. An example of an incentive within an incentive. I also stopped to see one company whose executives I had met socially over the weekend. This was in the interest of developing new business for the firm.

2:30 Arriving in the nick of time, my colleague and I met with the vice president of public and government relations for the Whirlpool Corporation, headquartered in Benton Harbor, Michigan. Whirlpool, the world's largest appliance maker, worked with us in a number of capacities: marketing public relations, media relations in Washington, DC, corporate public relations, and was using our facilities in arts and communications counseling and research. We are very proud of our association with Whirlpool, one of the country's best-managed companies. Public relations firms are judged by the company they keep, and being retained by Whirlpool is being in very good company.

We brainstormed—or exchanged creative ideas—on a possible Op Ed article for Whirlpool. Op Ed means opposite the editorial page, and these signed stories by various experts or company executives are effective means of expressing a company's viewpoint in its own words. A few months before this meeting, we had rewritten a speech on corporate philanthropy delivered by a top Whirlpool executive and arranged for it to be published opposite the editorial page in the *Chicago Tribune.* This time we decided to aim at the *New York Times, Wall Street Journal,* or "My Turn" column in *Newsweek.*

4:00 We then watch a film on Whirlpool's water conservation made by students at Andrews University in Michigan. It is a very good effort and will be useful when plant officials explain Whirlpool's interest in water in their communities.

4:15 Return phone calls and answer letters with resumes requesting employment.

4:30 Talk with public relations executive at *Chicago Sun-Times.* We are arranging a gathering using *Sun-Times* reporters as speakers for a meeting of corporate chief executives who belong to the Young Presidents Organization or Chief Executives Organization, for those who graduate from YPO at age forty-nine, the maximum age of members. We discuss a small detail and the *Sun-Times* executive says he'll check with his publisher and call me back.

4:45 Sign letters to media urging interviews of a client. Try to reach producer of WTTW-TV's *John Callaway Interviews* program, for same client. Leave message. She calls back when I am not there.

5:15 Read copy submitted by others: one press release, one letter. Write letter to a friend at Booz, Allen, Hamilton management consultants, sending him item in our newsletter discussing our graphic design work for his corporate headquarters in New York. My motive is informing him that what is done in New York might also be done in Chicago.

6:15 Clean up desk, which is full of papers, and leave the office. I read over a selection of magazines brought from the office. It's a diverse group, reflecting the different accounts I work on: *Stereo Review, Audio,* and *Public Relations Journal.* It's been a busy day.

OPPORTUNITIES TO LEARN ABOUT PUBLIC RELATIONS IN A SECRETARIAL POSITION

by Laurel Goldberg, former executive assistant to Morris B. Rotman

If you want to learn the many skills necessary for a job in public relations, start out as an assistant working with good public relations people.

Working with various executives who deal with different accounts, you pick up knowledge on a broad range of subjects and tips on how to present that knowledge in a clear, concise way. If you can absorb what you type, you learn what goes into a sales proposal, an outline for a new program, continuing work reports to clients, budgets, and pitch letters to the media. If you are lucky enough to work for a talented writer, you can see for yourself how an exciting lead paragraph can draw you into a letter and make you believe in the concept or company under discussion.

Assistants are liaisons between their bosses and clients or solicitors. You have to understand the needs of your bosses and be a buffer between them and the people wanting to talk to them. You have to give out the right information without telling too much. Finesse is developed in handling people over the phone or in person. As a public relations executive, a good phone personality helps in setting up media dates, and the skill of dealing with people cannot be stressed too much as a basic skill in public relations. The contacts made as an assistant can be continued as you progress to the executive level or perfect your skills.

Accuracy is one of an assistant's most important attributes. An error-free job of proofreading will win you praise when you save a client money because the copy for a brochure doesn't need to be corrected. Attention to all the details your bosses throw at you can be a good training ground for later work in public relations, when it is your responsibility to make sure all the divergent strands of an event or report come into place.

Administrative skills must be mastered before you think of learning the executive's job. That means knowing the rules of grammar and punctuation and how to spell, which will help if you eventually become a writer. Also, good assistants are expected to edit the copy they type. That doesn't give one free rein to change the tone or style of a letter or proposal, but it means correcting a word or two that is repeated too often or used in an incorrect manner. Being an assistant is one of the best ways to learn about the English language.

Design and presentation of materials are important in public relations. Assistants use words and layout whenever they arrange a letter on a page or organize a sales package. Working with suppliers to get a release printed acquaints you with design firms and typesetters. Making sure the printed material arrives on time helps you understand the importance of deadlines.

In this age of changing technology, assistants are the first in an office to learn about computer programs and audiovisual equipment. They are the people in the forefront of what a future office will be.

A good job will enable an assistant to contact hotels and restaurants to set up meetings, arrange travel schedules to conform to media tours, learn about research and reference manuals, become aware of the various ways to get materials somewhere in time, keep track of details, and acquire general knowledge on a variety of subjects. You can pick up the skills to handle people with ease and become able to change a load of papers, notes, and photographs into a package of understandable and good-looking material. You can become the type of person who can take information and present it in a way that can communicate its message. In other words, a public relations assistant can develop in the job to become the raw material needed for a good public relations executive.

JOB DESCRIPTIONS

Each public relations firm has a hierarchy within which an employee can advance. A beginner can join a firm as an assistant or an account assistant and be promoted up the ranks to account executive, account supervisor, vice president, and eventually senior vice president. Descriptions of these titles are as follows:

Account Assistant: Functions as an assistant to an account executive or account supervisor. Usually a person at entry level with little or no public relations experience and who receives close supervision.

Account Executive: Responsible for handling day-to-day activities of one or more accounts. Performs all traditional public relations functions including writing, media contact, and placement; client liaison; and support service supervision. Reports to account supervisor or higher executive.

Account Supervisor: Directs client programs and supervises other employees. Responsible for day-to-day account activities, preparation of client reports, work plans, supervision of account executives and assistants. Monitors out-of-pocket expenses and budgets of accounts, maintains client contacts, and tries to expand existing accounts. Probably involved in sales activities. A record of achievement must be present before an individual assumes this level of middle management. Reports to vice president or senior vice president, according to account.

Vice President: Assumes administrative responsibilities for accounts including budgeting, expense monitoring, profitability, and supervision of staff members. Demonstrates the ability to conduct account and other management responsibilities successfully with minimal supervision. Probably involved in sales activities, including program proposals, sales presentations, and expanding services to clients. This position is held by an individual who has demonstrated consistent management skills over a number of years and has potential for a senior position within the firm.

Senior Vice President: A group supervisor with ultimate responsibility for the success of profitability of a number of accounts. Responsible for managing the members of the group, reviewing their performance, and making recommendations to management. Routinely counsels clients and is heavily involved in new business activities, including program proposals and client presentations. A person in this position has demonstrated a substantial track record of successfully completed assignments, account supervision, professional and business management capabilities, sales skills, and employee supervision, and is expected to exhibit the highest standards of the profession in ability and experience.

TYPES OF PUBLIC RELATIONS PROJECTS

Within public relations, there are various types of communications programs that can be tailored to a client's objectives, such as projects dealing with:

Public information
Investor relations
Corporate communications
Public affairs
Marketing or product publicity
Consumer services
Research
Employee relations
Financial relations

On the following pages are checklists to help develop ideas for several of the above types of programs.

INVESTOR RELATIONS CHECKLIST

Investment Community Contact

Arrange meetings
Analyst society chapters
Analyst "splinter groups" of industry specialists
Specially selected groups
Brokers
Brokerage sales staffs
Institutional, bank, corporate, and insurance company
  portfolio managers
Investment advisors
One-on-one meetings

Preparation for meetings
Guest lists
Invitations
Facilities arrangements
Presentation outline or text
Audiovisual aids
Information kits
Tape and distribute presentation
Follow-up surveys
Related publicity

International
United Kingdom
Paris
Tokyo

Frankfurt
Geneva
Zurich

Finding new investors among
Satisfied customers
Employees
Existing shareholders/friends
Distributors
Dealers
Former shareholders
Plant neighbors

Dividend mailings

Dividend inserts

Inquiry-handling-systems form letters

Shareholder surveys

Advertising

Financial
Annual reports
Interim results
Annual results
Corporate news

Corporate
Image-building campaign
Required announcements
Corporate philosophy

Shareholder Relations

Annual and interim shareholder reports
 Concept
 Design
 Writing
 Production
 Photography
 Readership studies
 Advertising
 Distribution
 Evaluation

Special reports
 Preliminary year-end results
 Corporate actions such as acquisitions, new facilities
 Market expansion
 Diversification moves
 Financial newsletters
 Labor contract actions

Annual meetings
 Physical arrangements
 Special shareholder invitations
 Press attendance
 Analyst attendance
 Speeches
 Audiovisual requirements
 Management rehearsals

Difficult questions and answers
Special press interviews
Product demonstrations, displays
Post meeting reports to shareholder
Facilities tour
Evaluations

New shareholder materials
Welcome letter
Information packet
Studies
Sample product distribution

Printed materials
Fact books for analysts
Corporate brochures
Speech reprints
Status reports
Advertising and publicity
Reprints

Opinion surveys

Analyst's visits to company facilities

Investment community mailing lists
Development (national or international)
Maintenance
Updating

Continuing firsthand contacts
Wall Street
LaSalle Street

West Coast
Other key financial centers

Investors show participation
Arrange exhibits
Staff exhibits, distribute corporate printed materials
Presentations

Company Publicity

Required disclosures
Sales, earnings
Acquisitions or divestitures
Dividend actions
Product and/or research breakthroughs
Major management changes

Feature publicity
Newspaper interviews
Articles in financial, business journals
Major trade media articles
Wire service interviews
Radio and TV interviews

Corporate news
Price changes
Environmental protection
International expansion
Awards and honors

MARKETING SERVICES CHECKLIST

Consumer Publicity

Created special events
Press kits
Editorial briefings
News and feature releases
Picture articles
Wire service, feature syndicate stories
Contact with freelance writers and columnists
Mat releases, clip sheets
TV, radio appearances
TV newsclips, scripts
Radio tapes, scripts
Business and financial page publicity
Product sampling of influentials
Products on TV shows, in movies
Test market programs
Key market publicity tours
  Development of themes
  Selection, training, rehearsing spokespersons
  Scheduling interviews
  Accompaniment on tour
  Merchandising publicity results
Films, videotapes

Counsel

Public relations audits
Evaluating marketing problems, programs
Opinion surveys, market research
Consumer attitudes, trends
Government relations

Created Marketing Tools

Brochures, booklets, leaflets, fact sheets
Sales kits
Newsletters (external, internal)
Sales presentations
Films, slides, videotapes
Distributor, dealer, sales force special events
Audiovisuals
User/sales training materials
Point-of-sale support (posters, counter cards, shelf-talkers,
    etc.)
Premium programs
Advertising specialties
Direct mail
Exhibits and displays
Product demonstrations
Product photos, graphics
Publicity reprints
Catalogs, catalog sheets
Web page

Promotional Programs

Creation of special events
Contests, sweepstakes
Tie-ins with advertising
Co-op programs with other companies, organizations

Trade and Industry Relations

News releases
Exclusive articles
   Company/product profiles
   User/dealer case studies
   Industry trend features
   "How to" merchandising stories
   Opinion pieces, guest editorials on major industry issues
Other trade publicity
   New product introductions
   Sales activities, personnel moves, distributor
      appointments
   Newsworthy photographs
   Advertising, marketing plans
   New literature
   Special trade supplements
Speeches before industry groups
   Research, writing

Rehearsing speakers on videotape
Audiovisuals
Publicity
Customer seminars
Trade shows, conventions
Exhibits, displays
Liaison with trade groups

Government, Consumerism

Early warning on emerging issues (Washington,
    state levels)
Monitoring pending legislation
Liaison with consumer groups
Briefings for government officials, consumerists, press
Reviewing, evaluating press coverage
Position papers
Appearances before government bodies (FTC, CPSC,
    OSHA, FDA, Congress, state and local governments)
    Arrangements to appear
    Assisting with testimony
    Submitting statements
    Publicizing remarks
Issue-oriented advertising
Public service broadcast announcements

Special Interest Groups

Programs designed for:
Educators
Students, youth
Extension agents
Government officials
Management consultants
Home economists
Women's clubs
Men's service clubs
Professionals (doctors, lawyers, accountants, etc.)
Churches, clergy
Charitable, other nonprofit organizations
Trade groups

RESEARCH SERVICES CHECKLIST

Retrieve information on a company or on any subject.
Monitor press coverage and awareness of an industry or
issue.
Develop data for a speech, report, memo, or sales proposal.
Profile companies, industries, or an individual.
Investigate a market or an industry and compile existing
market data.
Prepare bibliographies.
Report on economic trends.

Provide general information about legal situations.
Check the progress of proposed legislation.
Formulate political campaign issue papers.
Obtain background for advertising, public relations, or sales promotion programs.
Request detailed data from specialized and technical libraries or from experts.

EMPLOYEE RELATIONS CHECKLIST

Assemble and analyze information about a company's structure and how it affects internal communications.
Find out what management sees as organizational needs and what the employees feel are important, and define as a set of communications objectives.
Counsel on the use of specific communications techniques and tools and make sure they are properly used in terms of priority and budget. This includes: publications, audiovisual devices, meeting arrangements, and publicity and advertising.
Critique methods currently used to communicate with employees.
Research public attitudes that may influence employees.
Counsel on staffing the employee communications function.

FIELDS OF PUBLIC RELATIONS*

Business Corporations. The greatest amount of public relations activity will be found in business and industry.

Associations. There are more than 14,000 active national associations, the majority of which are headquartered in New York City, Washington, DC, or Chicago. Associations are not engaged directly in the marketing of products, but rather in creating a favorable climate for an industry or a cause.

Similar activities are maintained by information bureaus, institutions, councils, and foundations, which frequently derive support from business and industry and are devoted to matters of public concern, such as conservation, safety, and nutrition.

Professional societies, both national and regional, also have their public relations activities organized on lines similar to trade membership groups. Legal and medical groups are examples.

---

*From "Careers in Public Relations" (New York: Public Relations Society of America, Inc.).

Labor Unions. Trade unions, like the businesses that employ their members, recognize the importance of building public support for their positions and programs. The AFL-CIO, many of its affiliated unions, and major independent unions at the international or national, state, and local levels operate news bureaus, sponsor radio and television programs, offer films and educational programs to schools and civic groups, organize speakers' bureaus, and publish a variety of newspapers, brochures, and other materials. Public relations people who start in the labor movement tend to remain in this field throughout their careers.

Public Relations Firms. Most public relations firms or counselors are located in large metropolitan centers, with heavy concentration in New York City and Chicago. Public relations firms range in staff size from several employing nearly a thousand people to the great majority with fewer than a dozen workers. There is hardly any kind of public relations job that is not handled by consulting firms. Some specialize in financial or investor relations, government relations, employee communications, education and social programs, or industrial products or consumer marketing programs. The great majority have varied accounts. In some instances, they offer advertising as well as public relations services.

Schools and Colleges. Few institutions of higher learning are without organized public relations activities, which are frequently combined with "development" or fund-raising for the institution. Though fund-raising itself is a specialized field, a number of the tools used, including brochures, letters, and special events, are similar to those used in other public relations work. Large colleges and universities may have offices of public relations for information separate from the development department. These offices will handle press relations, community relations, special observances, speakers' bureaus, and speech writing and other typical public relations activities. Publications, including the school catalog, descriptive brochures, bulletins, and news publications are frequently an important part of the communications function.

More and more secondary schools and school systems are also undertaking organized public relations programs. Cultural institutions, such as museums, historical societies, musical organizations, art councils, theaters, and libraries also employ public relations personnel to further their ends.

Volunteer Agencies. Sometimes called the nonprofit, public service, or social sector, voluntary agencies include those in the health and welfare field involved with rehabilitation, recreation, and family service. Another segment is the hospital field, which provides work opportunity in press, community, and patron relations as well as in fund-raising. Other service organizations, including the Red Cross, Girl Scouts, Young Men's Christian Association (YMCA), along with religious, community, and special fund organizations and fraternal groups, also use public relations for acceptance and support.

Government. Government units, including those of the armed forces, designate their public relations activity as "public information." In addition to the numerous federal agencies, commissions, and other bodies that have press and information officers, state, regional, county, and municipal units are also staffed with persons responsible for good relations with the public and for reporting on their organizations' activities. On the international level, the United States Information Agency (USIA) is charged with informing people outside our country about our ideals and the operation of the American system.

WHERE TO STUDY PUBLIC RELATIONS*

Following is an excerpted list of public relations academic programs available at education institutions throughout the United States. The list was compiled by the Public Relations Society of America, Inc., 33 Irving Place, New York, NY 10003-2376; www.prsa.org.

Because growth in the field is ongoing, formal education sources are increasing. When you are ready to look for a school, you should contact the Foundation for Public Relations Research and Education, the Public Relations Society of America, or the individual schools themselves to get the most recent information. It is necessary to assume that school listings and schedules will change each quarter or semester. If you are considering full-time enrollment you will want to begin your requests for information at least a year in advance, and keep on checking on the latest developments even up until classes begin.

---

*From *Where Shall I Go to Study Public Relations?*

ALABAMA

Auburn University
Journalism Department
Auburn University, AL
36849-5206
B.A. Journalism, B.A.
Corporate Journalism

University of Alabama
College of Communication
& Information Sciences
Tuscaloosa, AL 35487-0172
B.A. Communication &
Information Sciences,
M.A. Communication &
Information Sciences

ALASKA

University of Alaska,
Anchorage
Department of Journalism
and Public
Communications
3211 Providence Drive
Anchorage, AK 99508
B.A. Journalism

University of Alaska, Fairbanks
Department of Journalism
and Broadcasting
P.O. Box 756120
101 Bunnell
Fairbanks, AK 99775-6120
B.A. Journalism

ARIZONA

Arizona State University
Walter Cronkite School of
Journalism and
Telecommunication
Tempe, AZ 85287-1305
B.A. Journalism,
B.A. Broadcasting, M.M.C.
Mass Communication

University of Arizona
Department of Journalism
Tucson, AZ 85721
B.A. Journalism

ARKANSAS

Arkansas State University
College of Communications
P.O. Box 540
State University, AR 72467-
0540
B.S. Journalism, Radio-TV

University of Arkansas,
Fayetteville
Department of Journalism
Fayetteville, AR 72701-1201
B.A. Journalism, M.A.
Journalism

University of Arkansas, Little
Rock
Department of Journalism
Little Rock, AR 72204
B.A. Journalism

CALIFORNIA

California Polytechnic State
  University
Department of Journalism
San Luis Obispo, CA 93407
B.S. Journalism

California State University,
  Chico
Department of Journalism
207 Tehama Hall
Chico, CA 95929-0600
B.A. Journalism

California State University,
  Fresno
Department of Mass
  Communication and
  Journalism
2225 E. San Ramon M/S 10
Fresno, CA 93740-8029
B.A. Mass Communication
  and Journalism, M.A.
  Mass Communication

California State University,
  Fullerton
Department of
  Communications
800 N. State College Blvd.
Fullerton, CA 92834-6846
B.A. Communications

California State University,
  Northridge
Department of Journalism
18111 Nordhoff St.
Northridge, CA 91330-8311
B.A. Journalism, M.A.
  Mass Communication

San Francisco State University
Department of Journalism
1600 Holloway Avenue
San Francisco, CA 94132
B.A. Journalism

San Jose State University
School of Journalism and
  Mass Communications
San Jose, CA 95192-0055
B.S. Journalism, B.S.
  Advertising, B.S. Public
  Relations, M.S. Mass
  Communications

University of California
Graduate School of
  Journalism
121 North Gate Hall #5860
Berkeley, CA 94720-5860
M.J. Journalism

University of Southern
California
School of Journalism
3502 Watt Way, ASC 325
Los Angeles, CA 90089-
0281
B.A. Broadcast Journalism,
B.A. Print Journalism,
B.A. Public Relations,
B.A. Journalism/East
Asian Area Studies, M.A.
Broadcast Journalism,
M.A. Print Journalism,
M.A. Strategic Public
Relations, M.A.
International Journalism

COLORADO

Colorado State University
Department of Journalism
and Technical
Communication
Fort Collins, CO 80523
B.A. Journalism

University of Colorado
School of Journalism and
Mass Communication
Campus Box 478
Boulder, CO 80309
B.S. Journalism, M.A.
Journalism

DISTRICT OF COLUMBIA

American University
School of Communication
Washington, DC 20016-
8017
B.A. Communication:
Journalism, B.A.
Communication: Public
Communication, M.A.
Journalism and Public
Affairs, M.A. Public
Communication

Howard University
Department of Journalism
Washington, DC 20059
B.A. Journalism
Department of Radio-TV-
Film
B.A. Broadcast Production
and Telecommunications
Management

FLORIDA

Florida A&M University
Division of Journalism
Tallahassee, FL 32307
B.S. Journalism

Florida International University
School of Journalism and
  Mass Communication
North Miami, FL 33181
B.S. Communication, M.S.
  Mass Communication

University of Florida
College of Journalism and
  Communications
Gainesville, FL 32611-8400
B.S. Journalism, B.S.
  Advertising, B.S.
  Telecommunication, B.S.
  Public Relations, M.A.
  Mass Communication

University of Miami
School of Communication
Coral Gables, FL 33124-
  2030
B.S. Communication, M.A.
  Journalism

University of South Florida
School of Mass
  Communications
4202 E. Fowler Ñ CIS 1040
Tampa, FL 33620
B.A. Mass Communications,
  M.A. Mass
  Communications

GEORGIA

University of Georgia
Henry W. Grady College of
  Journalism and Mass
  Communication
Athens, GA 30602-3018
A.B.J. Journalism, M.A.
  Journalism, Master of
  Mass Communication

HAWAII

University of Hawaii at Manoa
Department of Journalism
Honolulu, HI 96822-2217
B.A. Journalism

ILLINOIS

Eastern Illinois University
Department of Journalism
600 Lincoln Ave.
Charleston, IL 61920-3099
B.A. Journalism

Northwestern University
Medill School of Journalism
Fisk Hall, 1845 Sheridan Rd.
Evanston, IL 60208
B.S. Journalism, M.S.
  Integrated Marketing
  Communications, M.S.
  Journalism

Southern Illinois University,
Carbondale
School of Journalism
Carbondale, IL 62901-6601
B.S. Journalism

University of Illinois at
Urbana-Champaign
College of Communications
810 S. Wright St.
Urbana, IL 61801
B.S. Advertising, B.S. Media
Studies, B.S. Journalism
including Broadcast
Journalism, M.S.
Advertising, M.S.
Journalism including
Broadcast Journalism

INDIANA

Ball State University
Department of Journalism
Muncie, IN 47306
B.A. Journalism, B.S.
Journalism, B.A.
Advertising, B.S.
Advertising, B.A. Public
Relations, B.S. Public
Relations

Indiana University
School of Journalism
Bloomington, IN 47405
B.A.J., M.A. Professional

IOWA

Drake University
School of Journalism and
Mass Communication
Des Moines, IA 50311
B.A. Journalism and Mass
Communication

Iowa State University of
Science and Technology
Greenlee School of
Journalism and
Communication
Ames, IA 50011
B.A. Journalism and Mass
Communication
(including Electronic
Media Studies), B.A.
Advertising, B.S.
Journalism and Mass
Communication
(including Science
Communication),
M.S. Journalism and Mass
Communication

University of Iowa
School of Journalism and
Mass Communication
Iowa City, IA 52242
B.A. Journalism, B.S.
Journalism, M.A.
Professional

KANSAS

Kansas State University
A.Q. Miller School of
Journalism and Mass
Communications
Manhattan, KS 66506
B.A. Mass Communications,
B.S. Mass
Communications, M.S.
Mass Communications

University of Kansas
William Allen White School
of Journalism and Mass
Communications
Lawrence, KS 66045
B.S. Journalism, M.S.
Journalism

KENTUCKY

Murray State University
Department of Journalism
and Mass
Communications
Box 9
Murray, KY 42071-0009
B.A., B.S. Journalism,
Advertising, Public
Relations, and Radio-TV

Western Kentucky University
School of Journalism and
Broadcasting
Bowling Green, KY 42101-
3576
B.A. Advertising, B.A.
Photojournalism, B.A.
Print Journalism, B.A.
Public Relations

University of Kentucky
School of Journalism and
Telecommunications
Lexington, KY 40506-0042
B.A. or B.S.
Communications
(Journalism, Integrated
Strategic Communication,
Telecommunications)

LOUISIANA

Grambling State University
Department of Mass
Communication
P.O. Box 45
Grambling, LA 71245
B.A. Mass Communication

Louisiana State University
Manship School of Mass
Communication
Baton Rouge, LA 70803
B.A.M.C., M.M.C.

McNeese State University
Department of Mass
Communication
Lake Charles, LA 70609-
0335
B.S. Mass Communication

Nicholls State University
Department of Mass
Communication
Thibodaux, LA 70310
B.A. Mass Communication

Northwestern State University
Department of Journalism
P.O. Box 5273
Natchitoches, LA 71497
B.A. Journalism

Southern University
Department of Mass
Communications
Baton Rouge, LA 70813
B.A. Journalism, M.A.
Journalism

University of Louisiana at
Lafayette
Department of
Communication
P.O. Box 43650
Lafayette, LA 70504-3650
B.A., M.S.

University of Louisiana at
Monroe
Department of Mass
Communications
Monroe, LA 71209-0322
B.A. Journalism; B.A.
Radio, Television, and
Film, B.A.
Photojournalism

MARYLAND

University of Maryland
College of Journalism
College Park, MD 20742
B.A. Journalism, M.A.
Journalism

MICHIGAN

Central Michigan University
Department of Journalism
Mount Pleasant, MI 48859
B.A. Journalism, B.S.
Journalism

Michigan State University
School of Journalism
East Lansing, MI 48824-
1212
B.A. Journalism, M.A.
Journalism

MINNESOTA

St. Cloud State University
Department of Mass
Communications
St. Cloud, MN 56301-4498
B.S. Mass Communications,
M.S. Mass
Communications

University of Minnesota
School of Journalism and
Mass Communication
Minneapolis, MN 55455-
0418
B.A. Journalism-
Professional Program

MISSISSIPPI

Jackson State University
Department of Mass
Communications
P.O. Box 18590
Jackson, MS 39217
B.S. Mass Communications,
M.S. Mass
Communications

University of Mississippi
Department of Journalism
University, MS 38677-1848
B.A. Journalism, B.A.
Radio/Television

University of Southern
Mississippi
Department of Journalism
Box 5121
Hattiesburg, MS 39406-5121
B.A. Journalism, B.A.
Advertising

MISSOURI

University of Missouri-
Columbia
School of Journalism
103 Neff Hall
Columbia, MO 65211
B.J. Journalism, M.A.
Journalism

MONTANA

The University of Montana
School of Journalism
Missoula, MT 59812
B.A. Journalism, B.A.
Radio-Television, M.A.
Journalism

NEBRASKA

University of Nebraska
College of Journalism and
Mass Communications
Lincoln, NE 68588-0127
B.J. Journalism

NEVADA

University of Nevada-Reno
  Donald W. Reynolds School
    of Journalism
  Reno, NV 89557-0040
  B.A. Journalism, M.A.
    Journalism

NEW MEXICO

New Mexico State University
  Department of Journalism
    and Mass
    Communications
  MSC 3J, P.O. Box 30001
  Las Cruces, NM 88003-8001
  B.A. Journalism

University of New Mexico
  Department of
    Communication and
    Journalism
  Albuquerque, NM 87131-
    1171
  B.A. Journalism, B.A.
    Communication

NEW YORK

Columbia University
  Graduate School of
    Journalism
  New York, NY 10027
  M.S. Journalism

New York University
  Department of Journalism
    and Mass Communication
  10 Washington Place
  New York, NY 10003
  B.A. Journalism, M.A.
    Journalism (broadcast,
    newspaper, magazine,
    cultural reporting, and
    criticism sequences),
    M.A. in Journalism and
    Latin American-
    Caribbean Studies, M.A.
    in Business and Economic
    Reporting, M.A. in
    Journalism and French,
    M.A./M.S. in Biomedical
    Journalism, M.A. in
    Science and
    Environmental Reporting,
    M.A. in Journalism and
    Near Eastern Studies

Syracuse University
  S.I. Newhouse School of
    Public Communications
  Syracuse, NY 13244
  B.S. Public
    Communications, M.A.
    Public Communications,
    M.S. Public
    Communications

NORTH CAROLINA

University of North Carolina
School of Journalism and
Mass Communication
Chapel Hill, NC 27599-3365
A.B. Journalism and Mass
Communication, M.A.
Journalism and Mass
Communication

OHIO

Bowling Green State
University
Department of Journalism
Bowling Green, OH 43403
B.S. Journalism

Kent State University
School of Journalism and
Mass Communication
Kent, OH 44242-0001
B.A. Journalism and Mass
Communication, B.S.
Journalism and Mass
Communication, M.A.
Journalism and Mass
Communication

Ohio State University
School of Journalism and
Communication
Columbus, OH 43210-1339
B.A.J. Journalism, M.A.
Journalism

Ohio University
E.W. Scripps School of
Journalism
Athens, OH 45701
B.S.J. Journalism, M.S.J.
Journalism

OKLAHOMA

Oklahoma State University
School of Journalism and
Broadcasting
Stillwater, OK 74078-0195
B.S. and B.A. Journalism

University of Oklahoma
Gaylord College of
Journalism and Mass
Communication
Norman, OK 73019
B.A. Journalism, M.A.
Journalism and Mass
Communication

OREGON

University of Oregon
School of Journalism and
Communication
1275 University of Oregon
Eugene, OR 97403-1275
B.A. Journalism, B.S.
Journalism, M.A.
Journalism, M.S.
Journalism

PENNSYLVANIA

Pennsylvania State University
College of Communications
201 Carnegie Bldg.
University Park, PA 16802
B.A. Journalism, B.A. Film/
Video, B.A. Advertising/
Public Relations, B.A.
Telecommunications,
B.A. Media Studies, M.A.
Telecommunications
Studies

Temple University
Department of Journalism,
Public Relations, and
Advertising
Philadelphia, PA 19122
B.A. Journalism, M.J.
Journalism

SOUTH CAROLINA

University of South Carolina
College of Journalism and
Mass Communications
Columbia, SC 29208
B.A. Journalism, M.M.C.,
M.A.

Winthrop University
Department of Mass
Communication
Rock Hill, SC 29733-0001
B.A. Broadcasting, B.A.
Journalism

SOUTH DAKOTA

South Dakota State University
Department of Journalism
and Mass Communication
Brookings, SD 57007
B.S. Journalism, B.A.
Journalism

University of South Dakota
Department of Mass
Communication
Vermillion, SD 57069-2390
B.A. Mass Communication,
B.S. Mass
Communication

TENNESSEE

East Tennessee State
University
Department of
Communication
Johnson City, TN 37614-
0667
B.A. Mass Communications,
B.S. Mass
Communications

Middle Tennessee State
  University
  College of Mass
  Communication
  Murfreesboro, TN 37132
  B.S. Mass Communication,
  M.S. Mass
  Communication

University of Memphis
  Department of Journalism
  Memphis, TN 38152
  B.A. Journalism, M.A.
  Journalism

University of Tennessee
  College of Communications
  Knoxville, TN 37996-0332
  B.S. Communications, M.S.
  Communications

University of Tennessee at
  Chattanooga
  Department of
  Communication
  Chattanooga, TN 37403-
  2598
  B.A. Communication

University of Tennessee at
  Martin
  Department of
  Communications
  Martin, TN 38238-5099
  B.A., B.S., Public Relations

TEXAS

Baylor University
  Department of Journalism
  P.O. Box 97353
  Waco, TX 76798-7353
  B.A. Journalism

Texas A&M University
  Department of Journalism
  College Station, TX 77843-
  4111
  B.A. Journalism, B.S.
  Journalism, B.S.
  Agricultural Journalism

Texas Christian University
  Department of Journalism
  TCU Box 298060
  Ft. Worth, TX 76129
  B.A. News-Editorial
  Journalism, International
  Communication, B.S.
  News-Editorial
  Journalism, Advertising-
  Public Relations,
  Broadcast Journalism,
  M.S. Journalism

Texas Tech University
  School of Mass
  Communications
  Lubbock, TX 79409-3082
  B.A. Journalism, B.A.
  Advertising, B.A. Public

Relations, B.A.
Telecommunications,
B.A.
Photocommunications

Texas Woman's University
Program in Mass
Communications
P.O. Box 425828
Denton, TX 76204-5828
B.S. Mass Communications,
B.A. Mass
Communications

University of North Texas
Department of Journalism
and Mayborn Graduate
Institute of Journalism
P.O. Box 311460
Denton, TX 76203-1460
B.A. Journalism, B.S.
Journalism, M.A.
Journalism, M.J.
Journalism

University of Texas
Department of Journalism
Austin, TX 78712
B.J. Journalism

UTAH

Brigham Young University
Department of
Communications
Room E509, Harris Fine
Arts Center
Provo, UT 84602-6404
B.A. Communications

University of Utah
Department of
Communication
255 S. Central Campus Dr.,
Room 2400
Salt Lake City, UT 84112
B.S. Mass Communication,
B.A. Mass
Communication, M.S.
Mass Communication,
M.A. Mass
Communication

VIRGINIA

Hampton University
Department of Mass Media
Arts
Hampton, VA 23668
B.A. Mass Media Arts

Norfolk State University
Department of Mass
Communications and
Journalism
Norfolk, VA 23504
B.A. Mass Communications,
B.S. Journalism

Washington and Lee University
Department of Journalism
and Mass
Communications
Lexington, VA 24450
B.A.

WASHINGTON

University of Washington
School of Communications
Box 353740
Seattle, WA 98195-3740
B.A. Arts and Sciences

WEST VIRGINIA

Marshall University
W. Page Pitt School of
Journalism and Mass
Communications
Huntington, WV 25755
B.A. Journalism, M.A.J.
Journalism

West Virginia University
Perley Isaac Reed School of
Journalism
Morgantown, WV 26506-
6010
B.S. Journalism, M.S.
Journalism

WISCONSIN

Marquette University
College of Communication
Milwaukee, WI 53201-1881
B.A. Advertising, Broadcast
and Electronic
Communication,
Journalism, Public
Relations, M.A.
Advertising, Broadcast
and Electronic
Communication,
Journalism, Public
Relations

University of Wisconsin-Eau
Claire
Department of
Communication and
Journalism
Eau Claire, WI 54702-4004
B.A., B.S., Communication

University of Wisconsin-
Oshkosh
Department of Journalism
Oshkosh, WI 54901-8696
B.A. Journalism, B.S.
Journalism

University of Wisconsin-River
Falls
Department of Journalism
River Falls, WI 54022
B.A. Journalism, B.S.
Journalism

INTERNATIONAL

Pontificia Universidad Católica
de Chile
School of Journalism
Avenida Jaime Guzmán
Errázuriz 3.300-
Providencia
Santiago, Chile
Licentiate in journalism,
professional title in
journalism

OFFICIAL STATEMENT ON PUBLIC RELATIONS

(Formally adopted by PRS Assembly, November 6, 1982.)

Public relations helps our complex, pluralistic society to reach decisions and function more effectively by contributing to mutual understanding among groups and institutions. It serves to bring private and public policies into harmony.

Public relations serves a wide variety of institutions in society such as businesses, trade unions, government agencies, voluntary associations, foundations, hospitals, and educational and religious institutions. To achieve their goals, these institutions must develop effective relationships with many different audiences or publics such as employees, members, customers, local communities, shareholders, and other institutions, and with society at large.

The managements of institutions need to understand the attitudes and values of their publics in order to achieve institutional goals. The goals themselves are shaped by the external environment. The public relations practitioner acts as a counselor to management, and as a mediator, helping to translate private aims into reasonable, publicly acceptable policy and action.

As a management function, public relations encompasses the following:

- Anticipating, analyzing, and interpreting public opinion, attitudes, and issues that might impact, for good or ill, the operations and plans of the organization.
- Counseling management at all levels in the organization with regard to policy decisions, courses of action, and communication, taking into account their public ramifications and the organization's social or citizenship responsibilities.
- Researching, conducting, and evaluating, on a continuing basis, programs of action and communication to achieve informed public understanding necessary to the success of an organization's aims. These may include marketing, financial, fund-raising, employee, community, or government relations and other programs.
- Planning and implementing the organization's efforts to influence or change public policy.
- Setting objectives, planning, budgeting, recruiting, and training staff, developing facilities—in short, managing the resources needed to perform all of the above.
- Having the knowledge that may be required in the professional practice of public relations. Examples of some of these areas of knowledge include communication arts, psychology, social psychology, sociology, political science, economics, and the principles of management

and ethics. Technical knowledge and skills are required for opinion research, public issues analysis, media relations, direct mail, institutional advertising, publications, film/video productions, special events, speeches, and presentations.

In helping to define and implement policy, the public relations practitioner utilizes a variety of professional communication skills and plays an integrative role both within the organization and between the organization and the external environment.